INVESTIGATING ENTREPRENEURIAL OPPORTUNITIES

ENTREPRENEURSHIP AND THE MANAGEMENT OF GROWING ENTERPRISES

A Sage Publication Series

THE ENTREPRENEURSHIP AND THE MANAGEMENT OF GROWING ENTERPRISES series focuses on leading edge and specialized ideas important to the creation and effective management of new businesses. Each volume provides in-depth, accessible, up-to-date information to graduate and advanced undergraduates students, investors, and entrepreneurs.

BOOKS IN THIS SERIES

INVESTIGATING ENTREPRENEURIAL OPPORTUNITIES

A Practical Guide for Due Diligence

RICHARD P. GREEN II

JAMES J. CARROLL

EMGE

Sage Publications, Inc.
International Educational and Professional Publisher
Thousand Oaks ▪ London ▪ New Delhi

For information:

Sage Publications, Inc.
2455 Teller Road
Thousand Oaks, California 91320
E-mail: order@sagepub.com

Sage Publications Ltd.
6 Bonhill Street
London EC2A 4PU
United Kingdom

Sage Publications India Pvt. Ltd.
M-32 Market
Greater Kailash I
New Delhi 110 048 India

Printed in the United States of America

Library of Congress Cataloging-in-Publication Data

Green, Richard P.
    Investigating entrepreneurial opportunities: A practical guide for due diligence / by Richard P. Green II and James J. Carroll.
        p. cm. — (Entrepreneurship and the management of growing enterprises)
    ISBN 0-8039-5941-9 (cloth: acid-free paper)
    ISBN 0-8039-5942-7 (pbk.: acid-free paper)
    1. Business enterprises—Purchasing—United States. 2. Disclosure of information—United States. 3. New business enterprises—United States. I. Carroll, James J. II. Title. III. Series.
    HD1393.4.U6 G73 2000
    658.1′6—dc21

99-050652

This book is printed on acid-free paper.

00 01 02 03 04 05 06 7 6 5 4 3 2 1

Acquisition Editor:	Marquita Flemming
Editorial Assistant:	MaryAnn Vail
Production Editor:	Sanford Robinson
Editorial Assistant:	Victoria Cheng
Typesetter:	Rebecca Evans
Indexer:	Teri Greenberg
Cover Designer:	Candice Harman

Contents

Introduction

In October 1989, Hendrix Niemann bought Automatic Door Specialists, Inc. The cork popped on a bottle of champagne. Toasts were offered to the success of the deal and the success of the business. "The next day," wrote Niemann, "I walked in the door of Automatic Door Specialists at 7:15 a.m. as the new owner" (1990, p. 38).

By June 1991, less than two years later, Niemann was broke. Bankruptcy seemed certain. "It was quite possible that everything, including our house, would be lost" (1991, p. 46).

So, what happened?

As Niemann discovered, operating your own business is a risky proposition. One invests personal funds, time, and energy in owning and operating a business, meanwhile foregoing other opportunities. At risk are one's wealth and self-esteem. Under the best of circumstances, the chance of failure is high. Under adverse business conditions, failure is nearly certain.

The best control for risk is to recognize and avoid bad purchase decisions through the process of *due diligence.* Due diligence comprises conducting an investigation to determine the full implications of acquiring a business. During the process of due diligence *every* aspect of the business is examined in exacting detail. Nothing is taken for granted. No statement is accepted without evidence, and all evidence is substantiated by sources external to the company.

Both the buyer and the seller should exercise due diligence prior to closing the sale or merger of a business. The buyer should attempt to ascertain that all facts about the business are known and that there will be no unpleasant surprises after the sale. The seller should seek assurances that the buyer is capable of meeting the terms of the purchase and should be certain to understand fully the tax consequences of the sale of the business.

In the United States, it is the buyer's responsibility to research a prospective purchase. A basic tenet of business law is *caveat emptor,* or, "Let the buyer beware." This does not mean that the seller can, with impunity, misrepresent the facts of the business; however, absent specific misrepresentations by the seller, the buyer assumes responsibility for understanding the condition and facts of the business. Thus the buyer, through the process of due diligence, attempts to determine exactly how the business is currently being operated and to substantiate (or to disprove) all representations made by the seller regarding the existence and value of assets, the extent of liabilities, and the financial performance and condition of the business.

Done correctly, due diligence simultaneously minimizes risk of failure by identifying the weaknesses of and threats to the business and developing strategies to overcome them, and maximizes the probability of business success by identifying the strengths and opportunities of the business and creating the structure to capitalize on them.

Finally, after a thorough and exacting investigation conducted with an attitude of informed skepticism, the would-be purchaser should sit down with business, financial, and legal advisors to evaluate the business and its chances of success under new ownership. Then, and only then, should a decision to purchase the business be made.

When done in this manner, due diligence is an activity that adds value to a business. However, completing this process does not—and cannot—guarantee success.

Hendrix Niemann did examine Automatic Door Specialists, Inc., with diligence. Indeed, as he reveals in a 1990 article, he uncovered several weaknesses in the business and numerous misrepresentations by the seller:

"Each of [the accountant's] findings was a punch in the stomach."

"The company was losing money . . . $36,000 for the first half of the fiscal year."

"It was likely the true loss year-to-date was close to $80,000."

"Sales for the year were down more than 50%."

"Close to half [of the receivables] were more than 90 days old, and the majority of that dated from [the previous year]."

"When the inventory was complete, it came in at 60% of its stated value on the balance sheet and $16,000 less than my accountant's worst-case scenario."

"Key lines were lost."

"Half the net worth of the company was gone."

"The parts and tools for installers and technicians were not replenished."

"Key people left and went to work for or started competing firms."

"The senior employee was aggrieved."

"I didn't have a sales manager."

"Customers were not taken care of."

"[The building] was a firetrap."

"The boiler was ancient and ready to blow."

"The seller couldn't be trusted."

So why would *anybody* buy a business in such an obvious state of mismanagement, obsolescence, disrepair, and competitive disadvantage, especially when the investigation has been so stressful and confusing?

Here's what Niemann wrote in 1990:

"I was terrified to go ahead with the deal for Automatic Door and terrified not to."

"I couldn't sort out the signals I was getting. Were these signs to walk away? Or just my finding out things that were going to be present in any business? Were they deal killers? Or just things that were going to affect the purchase price in *my* favor?"

"The Washington/Baltimore construction market was booming."

"The phone rang constantly with requests for bids."

"The access control/security systems industry was plenty healthy."

"[Key employees] clearly believed the company had a tremendous future—in different hands."

"We could feel confident that we knew everything it was humanly possible to know about the company."

"Automatic Door Specialists could thrive again."

"We would go ahead; but *only* if we got the right price."

So Niemann bought his business. And within two years faced bankruptcy and impoverishment.

What, if anything, was there that could have—*should* have—led him to make a different decision? What should any prospective purchaser of a business scrutinize or consider in making an acquisition decision? Were Niemann's business reversals due to incomplete information or due to an inappropriate decision in light of the information he collected?

Niemann admits that "buying a company that was losing money in an industry I knew nothing about, attempting to turn it around in a down economy, and trying all that with almost every personal asset I had in the world at stake, was perhaps not the smartest thing to do" (1991, p. 46). By his own words, Niemann's failure at due diligence came in part because he entered an industry of which he was ignorant, and so he failed to predict future economic conditions. His other failures at due diligence include the facts that (a) Niemann neither specifically identified nor pursued any competitive strengths of Automatic Door; (b) he failed to discover critical information concerning the competitive environment for Automatic Door's products and services; (c) he did not find or develop any new opportunities, but instead continued to chase business in which the company was losing money prior to his acquisition; and (d) he made the purchase of the business largely on emotional grounds: his severance pay from his former job was about to end, he was daunted by the prospect of performing yet another search for a business to acquire, and he felt that he could "rescue" the employees of Automatic Door, whom he had come to like and respect.

As a result of these failures, Niemann risked *everything* on an entrepreneurial venture that was currently hemorrhaging red ink.

The story of the purchase of Automatic Door illustrates a failure to exercise due diligence, and financial loss and psychological stress were the result. The purpose of this book is to provide insight into the *process of due diligence* that should be a major part of any potential business acquisition.

1 | An Overview of Investigation

The ultimate purpose of conducting an investigation, commonly called *due diligence,* is to develop information that allows one to make a reasonable estimate of the viability and future profitability of a business being considered for acquisition. It is not possible, however, to be certain of future business conditions and operations: The best that can be accomplished is to obtain the most accurate information possible, to make the best guesses possible of future business conditions, and to use the information and estimates to make a rational decision about the viability and desirability of a business.

Investigating a business, even a very small one, will produce huge amounts of data: sales information, product or service details, history, suppliers, customers, assets, liabilities, officers, employees, details of retirement obligations, contracts, leases. . . . The list seems endless. The task of the entrepreneur who would acquire a business is somehow to collect, assemble, and organize this huge amount of data, transforming it into information: information that is useful in making a purchase decision.

This chapter discusses the general processes that are utilized to find, collect, collate, and organize business data into information.

THE POSITION OF DUE DILIGENCE IN THE PROCESS OF ACQUIRING A BUSINESS

When a business is about to change hands, either by purchase or acquisition, there is a clear order of steps that the new owner should follow:

1. Conduct extensive interviews with the sellers of the business.
2. Study the financial reports and other records of the business.
3. Make a personal examination of the business site or sites.
4. Interview customers of and suppliers for the business.
5. Develop a detailed business plan for the acquisition.
6. Negotiate an appropriate price for the business based on the business plan projections.
7. Obtain sufficient capital to purchase and operate the business.

The first five of the above steps constitute a process of investigation, the purpose of which is to find out every important detail that affects the value of the business. This investigation is commonly called *due diligence.* The term has specific meaning for accountants and lawyers, who may be involved in the process of acquiring a business. For these professionals, due diligence means conducting an exhaustive search and exercising the care, experience, and expertise that is required of professionals.

Although an individual who acquires a business has no specific legal requirement to act with due diligence, conducting an exhaustive investigation of the business is a requirement of good sense. An entrepreneur invests a great deal into the acquisition of a business, including the entrepreneur's wealth, time, and self-esteem. With so much at stake, exercising care to avoid making a bad investment is simply common sense. Therefore, throughout this book, the term *due diligence* is used to refer to the investigation process, regardless of whether the investigation is being made by professional business advisors or by an entrepreneur.

THE PROCESS OF DUE DILIGENCE
IN BUSINESS ACQUISITIONS

Investigating a business for potential acquisition is a painstaking process of (a) defining the immediate goal of the investigation, (b) developing a plan to acquire information relevant to that goal, (c) substantiating the information with sources external to the company being investigated, (d) organizing the information to aid understanding, and (e) evaluating the information to make a purchase decision. In a very real sense, the process of due diligence is an exhaustive audit of all aspects of the business under consideration, conducted with the explicit purpose of uncovering misrepresentation and fraud.

The ultimate purpose of such an investigation is to develop information that allows one to make a reasonable estimate of the viability and future profitability of a business. It is not possible ever to be certain of the future—certainly not of future business conditions and operations. The best that one can accomplish is to obtain the most accurate information possible, to make the best guesses possible of future business conditions, and to use the information and estimates to make a rational decision about the viability and desirability of a business.

Although the goal of the due diligence process is to *prove* the viability of a business under consideration, the process followed actually seeks to accomplish the opposite: Rather than attempting to prove that a business is a good purchase, due diligence attempts to prove that a business is a *bad* purchase. Data are collected and information is developed in a concerted effort to demonstrate that the business *should not* be considered for acquisition. A prospective purchaser should start with the assumption, "This business is a loser that cannot be salvaged." If information is developed that disproves this statement, then—and only then—should a business be acquired.

When the due diligence process is carefully and correctly completed, the prospective buyer has at hand all possible information upon which to evaluate the risks and rewards of purchasing a business. The decision of whether to buy any particular business should include a consideration both of what the entrepreneur will lose if the business fails and of the entrepreneur's ability to survive the failure of the business. The risks of the business must not be underestimated, as the costs of failure are high.

THE RISKS OF THE ENTREPRENEURIAL ENDEAVOR

An entrepreneur's personal money and ongoing financial investments are largely committed to the success of the business. But an entrepreneur invests much more than mere money in the business and gets in return much more than mere profit. In addition to cash, entrepreneurs invest large amounts of personal time at the expense of other career options, and this investment continues throughout the ownership of the business. Furthermore, entrepreneurs invest their personal pride, self-esteem, reputation, and creativity, and might also invest family money and family time. The return on an investment may also be measured not only in terms of money, but also in terms of the entrepreneur's personal fulfillment, improved lifestyle, desire to take risks successfully, and prestige.

Starting or buying a business is a complex task and the outcome is uncertain. The risk of failure for a small business is quite high, and the cost of failure, measured in the terms listed above, is enormous. Thus any entrepreneur, any potential purchaser of a business, is well advised to identify and control for the weaknesses and vulnerabilities of that business to minimize the many risks of doing business.

The best control for business risk is to make good decisions based on complete and accurate information. As Niemann's purchase of Automatic Door, Inc., demonstrates, decisions based upon incomplete information, emotional issues, and inaccurate projections are likely to lead to disastrous business outcomes.

INFORMED DECISIONS

An informed decision, based on complete and accurate information, is an entrepreneur's best protection against business loss. Reliable information can allow a person considering an entrepreneurial venture to anticipate the results of entering the business. By performing an exhaustive due diligence examination, an entrepreneur gathers and confirms relevant data about the business. The data are then summarized and organized, providing information about the business being considered for acquisition.

Information allows for informed decisions. A decision based on complete information is better than a decision based on incomplete information or emotional appeal. In other words, an evaluation founded on facts will more nearly approximate the reality of actually buying and running the business than will some romantic idea of what being in business entails. Complete information, skeptically evaluated, leads to informed decisions that lower the financial and personal risks of being an entrepreneur.

Information is composed of data that are appropriately summarized, organized, and presented. Even small businesses generate data in overwhelming quantity, and all humans are limited in their ability to process data. And so, to be useful, the data must be summarized and presented in some organized manner. For example, few managers, if any, can extract information from a listing of a business's sales for the prior year. However, if sales data are summarized into graphs or charts of monthly sales, sales by product line, and sales by area, information about the business's sales is made readily accessible.

BUSINESS PLAN FORMAT

The process of due diligence produces a huge quantity of data that, to enable a critical evaluation by the prospective purchaser, must be converted to information by being summarized and organized. Many methods of organization exist, such as tables of information, graphs, summaries, indexes, and outlines. One form of condensing and organizing business information with which all entrepreneurs are (or *should be*) familiar is the business plan. Because of its familiarity and wide acceptance by investors, lenders, and managers, the *prove viability* business plan is used as a model for organizing the data developed during the process of due diligence.

Several different approaches exist for developing and presenting business plans (see Fry & Stoner, 1985; Kahrs & Krek, 1998). These approaches are usually consistent with the purpose of the plan. The approaches include the following six plans:

1. *The general strategic plan.* A general strategic business plan is used to develop long-range thinking. Plans of this type are used as thinking mechanisms for business owners and managers. The focus of these plans is to develop strategies for future implementation. This type of plan discusses product, market, and industry characteristics of the organization and its nearby competitors. The goal here is to develop a strategy. Plans of this type, however, fall short in the details of business operations.

2. *The budget basis plan.* Budget plans project business operations out over a few years. The first year is used as the basis of a budget for the business and its detailed operations. While more detailed than strategic plans, these plans lack strategic thinking and often do not consider the limits of the business in terms of its operational and personnel capacities (see Bradway & Pritehard, 1980).

3. *The calling card business plan.* Calling card business plans are *condensed* plans made of a specific set of succinct documents, including a description of the concept of the business, brief biographies of key officers and managers, and pro forma financial projections of limited depth. Such plans are used to ascertain if a venture capitalist has any interest in the project.

4. *The public relations business plan.* These business plans are used as general literature about an organization. They tend to be light on substance and long on presenting the organization in the most favorable way possible.

5. *The feasibility plan.* A feasibility plan is used to examine the risks and rewards of entering a new business, product, or service. As such, feasibility plans are usually extremely conservative, often based upon worst-case scenarios of marketing, manufacturing, distribution, and profit loss. These business plans are prepared in exacting detail and are supported with extensive economic and market analyses.

6. *The prove viability plan.* Proof of viability plans are used to obtain financing for a business from a bank or equity investor. A bank presentation would focus on the cash available for loan repayment and collateral available for debt coverage. An equity investor's business plan would focus on the future worth of the business in the securities market.

This book generally follows the prove viability business plan format, using both debt and equity perspectives. This dual perspective is important, because, as discussed above, the purpose of due diligence is to gather data not only to demonstrate that a candidate business is worthy of consideration, but also to disprove the proposition that the business is in all ways *unworthy* of being purchased. However, due diligence develops and considers more information than can be included in a prove viability business plan alone. The additional information generated concerns strategic, competitive, and quality issues. The approach of this book is to define the product as customers do, to specify exactly who constitutes the customer base, to determine the details of business operations in providing the goods or services to be sold, to test the capacities of facilities, and to determine detailed unit costs. These detailed items and concerns will create a more complete picture of the business than does any one business plan format. Although the emphasis here is upon proof of viability, the detailed information developed in the due diligence examination can be subsequently used to create a business plan in almost any format.

TARGETS OF THE DUE DILIGENCE PROCESS

The targets of the due diligence process are the aspects of a business that provide data useful in determining the future aspects of the business, which include just about anything that would interest the business owner and operator.

Although the specific targets of due diligence vary with the nature of the business being considered for acquisition, the investigative process always has the same goals, regardless of the nature of the business. First, the due diligence process attempts to find those things that an audit intended to disclose malfeasance would reveal: (a) fraud on the part of owners or managers; (b) misrepresentations made by the sellers, such as improperly recognized revenues or expenses; and (c) omitted information, such as unpaid taxes, pending or threatened litigation, or the technological obsolescence of the business's equipment, processes, product, or service. Second, the due diligence process searches for areas of inefficiency, unnoticed opportunities, waste, and mismanagement. The first goal of due diligence is to find information that, if found, would greatly affect the value of the business and the advisability of purchasing it. The second goal is to pinpoint areas where new owners can make immediate improvements to increase cash flows, profits, and the value of the business. Both set goals represent information that can provide a negotiating advantage for the potential buyer of a business.

There is no single route through the process of due diligence. One may start with any of the issues to be investigated and may complete the rest in any order that is convenient or practical. As a matter of practicality, however, the first information that an investigator usually receives is a set of the financial statements for the business being examined. This is done for many reasons: (a) The seller usually has financial statements available, and thus incurs little added cost in providing them to the prospective purchaser; (b) most entrepreneurs are familiar with financial statements, and thus can extract useful information from them; (c) financial statements tend to be accepted as representative of the business by investors; and (d) financial statements include many items that are considered to be indicators of future business results.

For these reasons, this book will be arranged to follow the overall format of an annual report of a public business, including the financial statements. The first section of the book, Chapters 2 through 4, deals with strategic issues. Chapters 5 through 8 explore operational issues. Chapters 9 through 14 look at financial issues: assets, liabilities, sales, revenues, expenses, profits, losses, and cash flow. The fourth section, Chapters 15 and 16, deal with issues of entrepreneurial endeavor and assigning a value to the business.

Within each section, specific due diligence targets will be discussed. Section one, on the strategic details of a business, will examine

- The nature of the market for the business's product and service
- A clear definition of what constitutes the business's product
- The competition within the market
- Any competitive advantage or disadvantage the business has
- A clear definition of who the business's customers are
- The specific strengths of the business being investigated
- The specific weaknesses of the business
- Any opportunities not currently being pursued
- Any threats to the business, such as onerous changes in regulation, new technologies, market saturation, or changing customer needs or fashions

Section two, on the operational details of a business, will look at

- The cost and process of making sales
- The cost of goods manufactured for sale
- The cost of purchased goods, both for internal use and for resale
- The cost of executives, managers, staff, and clerical employees
- The cost of labor
- The contractual terms of leases on property and equipment
- The adequacy and efficiency of production facilities and processes
- The reliability of essential suppliers
- Compliance with regulatory requirements, such as worker safety, handling of hazardous materials, and pollution abatement, and the cost of such compliance

The section of the book devoted to the financial aspects of the business will discuss

- The accuracy and reliability of financial statements—balance sheets, income statements, and statements of cash flow—provided by the selling owners and managers
- Estimates of the business's future earnings that will be available to the owners
- Economic and business factors that might cause the earnings to change rapidly
- The value of the business to outsiders in a subsequent sale
- The ability to quickly sell the business
- The timing and size of cash flows into and out of the business
- The sensitivity of earnings to certain internal and external forces, such as individual customers who account for significant percentages of sales
- Compliance with tax requirements, such as sales taxes, income taxes, property taxes, payroll taxes, and import/export duties and fees, and the cost of such compliance

In the last chapters of the book, we will examine personal issues of the entrepreneurial endeavor that affect entrepreneurial attractiveness, such as

- The quality of life for the owner-operator of a business: for example, the number and quality of hours in a typical workweek
- The nature of the work of an owner-operator
- The availability of job opportunities for family members in the business
- The approximate time and effort needed to develop the business for sale or for management by people other than the owner

This final section will also cover other information resulting from the discovery process. These items are far too numerous to mention, but may be even more valuable than those listed above.

A PROCESS OF INVESTIGATION

The information developed through the process of due diligence will be used to forecast the future of the business as the new owners will operate it. Much of this type of information is financial, and it is contained in financial statements prepared and provided by the sellers. Such financial statements include the common balance sheet, the income statement, and the statements of cash flows that are required of all publicly owned businesses. A prospective buyer should also examine the federal and state tax returns for prior years of the business's operations, including information forms for partnerships, S corporations, or limited liability companies.

All businesses, even the smallest, have at least some of these financial statements. However, all financial statements prepared by or for the selling owners and managers should be treated with great skepticism. The sellers have considerable motivation for presenting the business in the best possible manner to maximize the selling price. This can easily be done in small and large ways by manipulating the content, manner, and form of the financial statements. Accepting this information without further substantiation and investigation is entirely inadequate for the purpose of investigating a business acquisition. All financial statements are not created equally: Some are subjected to rigorous examination by professionals outside the business, others are dashed off by the owner at midnight on April 15! Regardless, no financial statement provided by the sellers should be accepted without question, inquiry, and investigation to substantiate its accuracy, completeness, and reliability.

Financial statements of businesses are created for differing reasons. These reasons affect the design and reliability of the statements, and their reliability for forecasting future financial conditions. Small business financial statements range from Schedule Cs, which are part of the personal income tax return of the owner, to formal financial statements prepared internally, to financial statements prepared by a professional accountant, to financial statements subjected to an audit by independent professional auditors.

Financial statements provided by the sellers are the starting place for due diligence. The statements must be examined exhaustively and substantiated by sources external to the business. The buyer should then adjust the amounts, contents, and format of the statements as indicated by the results of due diligence.

Thus an understanding of the purposes of specific financial statements and the process of preparing these financial statements is essential to due diligence. Within any set of financial statements are certain items that can be accepted without question, while other items are consistently biased, understated, or overstated.

Various types of financial statement are discussed below, in the order of the most reliable first, and the least reliable last.

Audited Financial Statements

Audited statements are the most reliable financial statements produced. Consistent application of generally accepted accounting principles (GAAP) are the hallmark of these audited statements. Independent professional auditors perform tests to establish the accuracy, completeness, and reliability of the statements that are prepared by the management of the business. The auditors attach a letter attesting that the statements fairly represent the business in GAAP terms. There is also a nearly perfect correlation between audited financial statements and the income tax returns for the business. If discrepancies between the two exist, a reconciliation is provided with the tax return.

The user of the statements may presume that the auditor of these statements has no financial stake in the company and was not paid to give a favorable opinion of the statements. This quality of independence from the data is central to the reliability of the information.

Disclosure notes to the financial statements are critical to a full appreciation of the statements. A good technique is to read the notes before reading the financial statements themselves. The quality of the information to be gleaned from an audited financial statement is greatly enhanced through an appreciation of the notes. For example, pending lawsuits against the company are described in the notes to the financial statements.

One drawback to audited financial statements is that GAAP has its own way of doing things. Information is presented in a manner intended to be informative to owners who are not actively engaged in the business. The information is highly condensed and is presented in a prescribed manner that divides important information between the formal financial statements and the often voluminous footnotes to the statements. Audited statements do, however, have two strong points for due diligence: First, a prospective buyer may place great reliance upon the auditors' work; and second, the matching principle of GAAP carefully segments revenue and associated costs and expense into the same accounting period, even if part of the transaction occurred in another accounting year. These two factors work to make it much more difficult for management to manipulate the income statement and statement of cash flows of the business.

The balance sheet of an audited statement, however, requires close examination during the process of due diligence. GAAP requires that all assets of the business be reported on the balance sheet at their original dollar cost at the time of purchase. This means, for example, that land and buildings are reported at the price that was paid for them, regardless of current value. Two identical properties may be reported at widely differing values, reflecting the original purchase price of each, not today's value. Thus even the crudest analysis requires a restatement of these values to something approximating current or future values (Pratt, 1989).

Internally developed (as opposed to purchased) intangible assets, such as patents, trademarks, customer lists, and name recognition, are not reported on the balance sheet. Intangibles, however, can be of enormous value: What, for example, is the value of the formula for Coca-Cola® or the value of the right to the name *Budweiser*®? Companies pay millions each year to maintain a strong image with consumers. Image is a key asset of the business, one that can be sold; however, the value of that image is not adequately represented on the balance sheet of the company.

Though the most reliable form of financial statement, audited financial statements are not *perfectly* reliable. The statements are prepared by managers hired to satisfy the reporting requirements of security exchanges, individual stockholders, and significant holders of debt. A major goal of reporting is not only to retain investors and debt-holders, but also to attract new ones. Investors and debt-holders prefer higher income and asset values to lower ones, because higher values enhance stock values and the likelihood of repayment of debt. Additionally, managers' compensation is often based upon financial statements of the firm. Thus managers have an incentive to manipulate the statements to overstate earnings and value. It is rare that a month goes by without a news report somewhere discussing fraudulent over-reporting of income to attract new stock market funding.

Reviewed Financial Statements

When the word *review* is found in the first line of the auditor's letter accompanying financial statements, the information contained in the statements is less reliable than that of audited financial statements. The audit firm is only claiming to have done a small part of the tests that are required for a full audit. In fact, the auditor's letter for reviewed statements says exactly that. Reviewed financial statements save the company money, as reviews are less costly than an audit. In general, reviewed statements are used by small businesses where belief in the integrity and reputation of the owner-manager is more important to other owners and to lenders than is a set of expensively audited statements.

Although the auditor does not affirm the fairness and reliability of the statements, the auditor does attest to the mathematical accuracy. Usually, the preparer of a reviewed statement advises the business owner concerning the adequacy of disclosure provided by the statements.

Compiled Financial Statements

Compiled financial statements are of still lower reliability than a reviewed statement. Compilations, as noted in the accountant's letter, are prepared from information furnished by the owner or manager and are only put into good accounting form by the accountant. No independent verification of the information is done by the accountant. In fact, financial statements are often compiled by company officers and owners. Although they may be competent to do this task, it seems unlikely that they will admit their own errors by preparing financial statements that reveal large inventory write-offs on poorly marketed products, or noncollected accounts receivable to companies to whom they granted credit.

Compiled financial statements may be viewed as possessing the quality expected of a good typist who transposes another's words: The words are spelled correctly, and punctuation is appropriate, but the page may be devoid of meaning. In the same way, a compiled statement should be free of arithmetical errors, and the income statement should follow the formula, *Revenues − costs = profits,* but the numbers may have no relationship to the operation of the business.

Small Business Income Tax Returns

All businesses are required to file an income tax return of one form or another (although some may not do so, in violation of federal law). Some businesses do not prepare formal financial statements, but rather rely on income tax returns to do the job of reporting to the outside world. There are several types of income tax reporting.

Stand-Alone Business Returns. In the United States, it is possible to create an artificial entity called a "C" corporation. A corporation is assumed to exist separately from the *owners* of the corporation. Such C corporations pay taxes on their profits and complete Federal Income Tax Return Form 1120, which is very similar to the individual 1040 form.

Another form of corporation, the S corporation, follows essentially the same form of reporting as does a C corporation; however, an S corporation does not pay taxes upon profits. Profit and loss are apportioned to the shareholders, who add their proportionate share of corporate profits to, or subtract their proportionate share of losses from, their individual income and are taxed upon the total.

Partnerships. Partnerships do not pay taxes. Rather, informational returns are prepared. The returns are filed with the IRS and furnished to each partner. As with S corporations, each partner then pays taxes on the pro-rata share of profit or loss.

Unincorporated Businesses. Profits and losses from unincorporated businesses or sole proprietorships are taxed as a part of the owner's personal income tax return. This is usually done on a Schedule C tax form as part of the owners' 1040 tax returns.

Non-Tax Filing Businesses. Businesses that do not file income tax returns violate U.S. law. There are a great number of these businesses. These businesses, as any other business, can be acquired. However, the person who acquires a business that is in violation of tax law may well be held liable for any unpaid taxes, interest, and penalties. The due diligence process, therefore, includes careful examination of the tax compliance of the target business. If the business is found to be noncompliant, the prospective purchaser will have to seek legal advice to remain free of liability for unpaid taxes.

Income tax returns are created to satisfy the reporting requirements of a tax authority, such as the IRS. These forms are usually completed in a manner calculated to lower the tax to be paid. This usually involves limiting income and maximizing reportable expenses. These manipulations are not necessarily either unethical or illegal. However, the practice does limit the value of tax returns as a source to evaluate a prospective acquisition. Subsequent chapters discuss ways the information from these data sources can be misleading and make specific recommendations to evaluate the information.

A SENSE OF INVESTIGATION

This chapter states that information about entrepreneurial opportunities may not always be reliable. Common sources of information, such as financial statements and tax returns, may be misleading, even when they are completely and accurately prepared. Each statement is prepared for a specific purpose, but none are intended specifically for the purpose of providing information to evaluate a business as an acquisition. In buying a business, the principal, "Let the buyer beware," holds with a vengeance. As was shown in the purchase of Automatic Door Specialists, Inc., a lack of wariness may lead to disaster. The best defense an entrepreneur has is to perform an exhaustive and exacting due diligence examination in which every assertion about a prospective business is independently substantiated.

SUGGESTED READINGS

Bazerman, M. (1998). *Judgment in managerial decision making.* New York: John Wiley & Sons.

Bernstein, L. A. (1998). *Financial statement analysis: Theory, application, and interpretation.* Boston: Irwin/McGraw-Hill.

Byrnes, J. P. (1998). *The nature and development of decision making: A self-regulation model.* Mahwah, NJ: Erlbaum.

Gumpert, D. E. (1996). *INC. magazine presents how to really create a successful business plan: Featuring the business plans of Pizza Hut, Software Publishing Corp., Celestial Seasonings, People Express, Ben & Jerry's.* Boston: Inc.

Jablonsky, S. F., & Barsky, N. P. (1998). *The manager's guide to financial statement analysis.* New York: John Wiley.

Lancaster, B. M. (1995). *Entrepreneurial training manual.* Monmouth Junction, NJ: Lancashire International.

Pinson, L., & Jinnett, J. (1996). *Anatomy of a business plan: A step-by-step guide to start smart, building the business and securing your company's future.* Chicago: Upstart.

Siegel, E. S., Ford, B. R., & Bornstein, J. M. (1993). *The Ernst & Young business plan guide.* New York: Wiley.

2 | Defining
the Enterprise

One might think that the definition of an enterprise is self-evident: After all, an airline provides air transportation, a sign company sells signs, and a tax preparation business does people's taxes, right?

Wrong!

In 1970, the managers of Trans World Airlines decided that the company wasn't an *airline,* it was a *transportation and relocation provider.* So, in the next few years TWA purchased Hilton International Hotels, Century 21 Real Estate, Canteen Corporation, and a large number of Hardee's franchises. Ted Turner decided that his highway sign business was in the information delivery industry. This definition led to the formation of Cable News Network (CNN). H & R Block, "The Income Tax People," defined their business as a *knowledge* business, and then acquired CompuServe, a major data service, predating the extensive use of the Internet. Block also acquired Personnel Pool of America, Path Management Industries, and Block Management Co. (Hoffer, 1987).

A reasonable question to ask, then, is, does the definition of the enterprise *really* matter? TWA, the airline, was subsequently spun-off by its acquired subsidiaries, which survived as TWA Services, Inc. (Alexander, Benson, & Gunderson, 1986). TWA, since being spun off, has passed through two changes in ownership and two bankruptcies, and has shrunk to half its former size. CNN, which brought us the 1991 Gulf War "live," has become a household word, and claims to be the most watched news program in the world. Turner is no longer in the outdoor advertising business, and has since redefined his television business, stating that the business of his company—which owns the TBS super channel, Cable News Network, CNN Headline News, CNN Radio, and Turner Program Services—"is . . . programming" (Hoard, 1985, p. 27). H & R Block, Inc., in a complicated three-way deal, sold "ailing" CompuServe to America Online and WorldCom in 1997 to "re-focus on core businesses" (Sandberg, 1997, p. 3).

Thus the short answer to our question is "Yes, the definition of the enterprise does matter!" It matters because it has an effect upon management decisions concerning businesses, product lines, marketing, and competitive strategy. Just as it matters for the large business examples above, it matters for small, entrepreneurial enterprises, perhaps even more so, given the high risk and high cost of failure of entrepreneurial businesses.

STRATEGIC VIEW

Without a doubt, a business has value as a possible entrepreneurial endeavor to the extent that it is able to fulfill future demands for its products or services. The business itself is often far more complex than can be described by any set of financial statements. Even before investigating the various components of a business, a prospective buyer must consider the overall strategic view. In the simplest terms, this means that the product or service offered by a business must meet a clearly defined consumer need. The business must provide its products or services in such manner that the company will make continuing profits or returns that are acceptable to the new owner.

Scope of Business: What Business Are We In?

The scope of a business refers to the self-imposed limits of the business, such as specific markets in which the business will compete, and the manner in which competition will be conducted. A scope statement is a carefully thought out definition of the limits that the business recognizes, including the principal products and markets served, and the nature of the service provided. Asking the question, "What business are we in?" is especially critical to understanding a business (Levitt, 1986).

Key components of a scope statement include the following:

1. A discussion of the business's principal products or services defined in terms of the specific *customer need* being satisfied by those goods or services. As businesses move to more service-based products, the definition of the customer need satisfied is critical to understanding a business. Although Levitt, as long ago as 1986, documented the strategic error of making business definitions based on function and not on customer need, current product definitions often fail to include customer need for by-products of business services. For example, telephone services often include extensive billing services. It may be the billing services that cause customers to select that telephone service. If so, the telephone provider should include *billing* as part of the product definition.

2. An analysis of brand names. Brand names affect industries in different ways. Brand names are typically more important in consumer products than in consumer services, such as hair cutting. Any product, even the most common of commodities, can be branded. Examples of successful branding of commodities include Tyson branded chickens and Evian or Perrier branded water. The effect of brand names in an industry must be part of the scope statement.

3. A discussion of the scope of the market served by a business. Market scope is identified by several boundaries: The more boundaries identified, the clearer and more efficient a marketing program becomes (Evans & Berman, 1994). A few typical market boundaries include
    a. Geographic considerations, including a city versus a rural location; location on an east-bound or west-bound highway, in a strip mall as opposed to downtown; being situated near a particular train station or within an airport; commuting distance. Is a truck service center, for example, located near an interstate highway? Is a surfboard retailer located near the ocean? (There are few, if any, retailers of surfboards in Kansas!)
    b. Demographics of personal customers, including age and gender, degree of proficiency with the type of product, income, marital status, and related items. An automotive repair shop, for example, might be marketed to consumers with older cars: Not only do new cars typically need few repairs, but they are also covered by warranties.

c. Demographics of industrial customers, including SIC codes; the type of industry a customer is involved in (manufacturer or reseller); the size of the company; the current owner of related items, such as toner cartridges for brand-name photocopiers; the overhead structure of a client company; and the degree of use of the product already. An example would be selling certified water-purity testing services to swimming pool and country club operators.

d. Marketing media. Because specifying the market scope is critical to the design of promotional campaigns, it is often useful to define market scope by the appropriate media reaching the desired customer. For example, a business might design a market approach aimed at industrial companies whose managers read the East Coast edition of the *Wall Street Journal*.

4. An examination of by-product sales. A particularly challenging issue is the sale of related products or by-products. A publishing company, for example, sells paperback novels. It may also sell advertising space in a few extra pages at the end of its books. Or consider photo processing operations that generate scrap silver, for which a ready market exists. These examples suggest profit opportunities in by-products. Profits are not always the case, however: By-products may also create unavoidable costs, as with quick lube operations, which generate contaminated oil that is expensive to dispose of.

ACQUISITION QUESTIONS

Once the scope of a business is clearly understood, the prospective purchaser must identify what, exactly, is being purchased with the business. The investigation of business scope may well reveal that the current owners either do not fully understand the business that they are attempting to sell, or are not effectively pursuing the full potential of the business. Certainly, a prospective purchaser hopes for such an eventuality. Finding areas where a business can be increased, improved, or made more efficient provides opportunities for new owners quickly to add value to the purchase.

On the other hand, there may be no missed opportunities that provide an immediate advantage for new owners. It is quite possible that the business is actually in a state of distress, which current owners are desperate to conceal. Thus the process of defining the enterprise includes (a) identifying who actually owns the business, (b) why the business is for sale, (c) what assets and liabilities are being transferred with the business, and (d) where the business assets are located.

Who Is the Seller of the Business?

Why should a prospective purchaser care who the seller of a business is? The buyer will own the business after the purchase is closed, so who cares who the seller might be?

The purchaser *should* care, in part because the purported seller may not be the actual owner or an authorized agent of the owner. Can you imagine "buying" a business from someone not authorized to sell it? The "seller" would accept your money and leave you with no business and no money. The seller's authority to make a sale is also an important consideration in partnership-type arrangements, in which the buyer must reach an agreement with more than one party. Nothing is more frustrating than trying to negotiate with all parties at once, being pushed back and forth between partners and shareholders who cannot agree on anything. Complicating the purchase even more is the need for any sale to be ratified by the corporation's shareholders. When purchasing a franchised business, a buyer must consider who is selling the business: the franchiser, an agent, or an unhappy current franchisee who is trying to escape an undesirable situation?

The right to sell can be identified in various ways, depending upon the business organization of the enterprise being acquired. All entrepreneurial businesses will be one of six forms of ownership: sole proprietorship, a partnership, a limited liability company (LLC), a C corporation, an S corporation, or a business held in an estate or trust.

Sole Proprietorship. If the business being considered is a sole proprietorship, the transaction, of necessity, consists of a purchase of assets. A business that is a sole proprietorship has no existence separate from its owner: It is *not* a legal entity. The acquisition can only consist of the purchase of assets and assumption of liabilities. Thus the most crucial issue is to determine that the seller actually owns the business. This can be approached by examining the seller's personal financial statements, business licenses, bank statements, leases, and income tax returns. It is important that any documents examined, including tax returns, be copies of the original. To gain this assurance, one may, with the seller's written permission, obtain copies of bank statements directly from the bank, of leases from the lessor, and of financial statements from the accountant who prepared them. Business licenses are on public record and can be examined at the appropriate government office. "As filed" income tax returns can be obtained from the seller's accountant or tax practitioner. Alternatively, copies of the seller's most recent tax return may be obtained from the Internal Revenue Service by having the seller sign a Form 4506, *Request for Copy or Transcript of Tax Form,* and submitting it to the IRS.

Because the business is not a legal entity separate from the owner and so is not an entity for which financial statements, bank accounts, and tax returns must be prepared, it is very common for owners of sole proprietorships to use funds freely for business and personal purposes. This makes analyzing the financial position of the business more difficult. It is essential to examine both the business's financial statements and the owner's income tax returns for the previous three to five years. One must examine, in detail, the owner's equity account for either excesses or shortages of owner draws, which are equivalent to salary. Excess draws may indicate that the owner is paying business expenses "off the books" to make the business appear to have a greater profit potential. The tax returns should be carefully examined for business expenses or capital assets that are not included in Schedule C, *Profit or Loss From Business,* but that are taken instead as personal deductions for the owner, either on Schedule A, *Itemized Deductions,* or on a separate Schedule C. Shortage of draws may indicate that the business is not generating sufficient cash flow for the owner to take money out of the business.

Owners who are trying to sell a business may also attempt to make the business look more profitable than it actually is by showing borrowed funds as income. To discover such misrepresentation, one must reconcile the Income Statement of the business to the owner's personal financial statement, and must review the details of reported interest expenses. It is unlikely that the owner will actually report borrowings as income on the tax return and pay the higher tax such misrepresentation would cause. Similarly, it is unlikely that any interest paid would not be deducted on the owner's income tax forms.

Partnerships and Limited Liability Companies. If the business being acquired is a partnership or LLC, it is owned by two or more persons who have agreed to conduct a business jointly for the purposes of making a profit. Though not legally required to do so, partnerships usually have written agreements that specify the profit and loss sharing of the partners. LLCs, which are treated as partnerships for tax purposes and as corporations for liability purposes, are required in all 50 states to have written agreements.

Most commonly, sales of partnerships and LLCs are structured to be bulk sales of the assets of the business, as *must* be the case in the sale of sole proprietorships. However, in the case of partnerships and LLCs, the business entity of the partnership may continue without interruption when a change in partners is made, if the partnership agreement specifies this is to be the case. Absent this provision in the partnership agreement, the partnership is legally dissolved whenever a change in partners occurs. Under all cases, if 50% or more of a partnership is sold, the partnership is terminated for tax purposes and a new partnership is established (see I.R.C. § 708[b][1][B]). This usually results in negative tax consequences for both seller and buyer. Any transfer, therefore, of 50% or more of a partnership or LLC must be considered carefully for its tax consequences. This is a highly technical matter requiring great expertise on the part of an accountant or tax practitioner.

Aside from tax considerations, the critical issue to be considered in purchasing a partnership or LLC is similar to that of proprietorships: Does the person purporting to sell the business have both legal ownership and the authority to sell? At the very least, the buyer should be furnished a copy of the partnership or LLC agreement. Better still, the buyer should require a sellers' statement in the purchase agreement stating that the sale has been approved and is in accordance with the provisions of the partnership or LLC agreement. The purchase agreement should be signed by the number of partners required to approve a sale, as specified in the partnership agreement.

C and S Corporations. Acquisitions of corporations may be structured either as a purchase of the entity—that is, as the purchase of stock—or as a purchase of assets. If the business entity is purchased, a careful investigation of contingent liabilities, especially lawsuits, must be made. Such an investigation is done, first, by carefully examining the minutes of the meetings of the board of directors, and second, by having one's attorney perform a search for pending litigation.

A copy of the articles of incorporation should be obtained from the records of the state in which the business was incorporated. Corporate bylaws, minutes, and the stock sale book should be maintained by the business and must be examined carefully by the prospective buyer. From these sources, one can ascertain the legal name of the corporation, the classes and numbers of outstanding stock, and the names of current corporate officers and directors. A perusal of these documents will disclose exactly what ownership rights are being purchased and will reveal the voting requirements necessary to approve a sale of the business.

The issues and documents for S corporations are the same as for C corporations, with a few differences. S corporations are limited to no more than 35 stockholders. Additionally, there are restrictions on the type of stock that may be issued by and on the type of entities who may be shareholders in S corporations (see I.R.C. § 1361).

Businesses Held in Trusts or Estates. The executor or administrator holds the title to businesses that have been transferred to estates. This person is legally responsible for administrating the financial dealings of the estate for the benefit of the beneficiaries. The executor or administrator is named in court documents called *letters testamentary* or *letters of administration.* The documents are public record and should be examined to verify that the person purporting to sell the business is indeed the named executor and thus has the authority to sell the business. It is not usually required to get the approval either of the court or of the beneficiaries to purchase a business from an estate, but it is prudent to do so, as it will greatly reduce the buyer's exposure to future litigation from the beneficiaries.

Legal title to businesses held in trusts is held by the trustee. The trustee is named in a legal document called a *trust agreement* or *trust indenture.* The considerations to be addressed by due diligence are the same for such businesses as for estates.

What Are the Owner's Motives for Selling the Business?

Determining the sellers' true motives for selling often requires a degree of clairvoyance. In fact, a purchaser may never be sure of *why* the current owners wish to sell. However, the personal intentions of the sellers can be a significant clue to the realities of the business. Here are a few possible intentions with negative consequences:

1. The owner is selling because the job of running the business is too demanding. A purchaser must determine the hours worked by the owner. If the hours are excessive, the seller should consider whether some of the work can be delegated to others while maintaining business profitability.

2. The owner wants to escape the difficulties of day-to-day management, while retaining a business relationship as either supplier or salesperson. A prospective purchaser of the business must be aware that such a relationship may take away the most profitable aspect of the business.

3. The owner does not really want to sell the business. The owner will take a down payment, and finance the balance of the purchase price anticipating that the buyer will fall into arrears on the loan. The former owner, richer by the amount of the down payment, can then foreclose, quickly step back in, take over, and continue in business as if it had never been sold.

It is normal for the seller to agree, as part of the sale, not to compete, within reasonable geographic, industry, and time limits, with the business. A part of the purchase price is usually allocated to pay for the noncompetition agreement. It is usually not desirable for the previous owner to be able to open up a competing business across the street from the business just sold.

What Are the Assets and Liabilities of the Business?

A full discussion of the investigation of the assets and liabilities to be acquired with the business is contained in Chapters 10 through 13. Consistent with the goal of defining what constitutes the enterprise, only the *types* of assets and liabilities that may be included in the purchase of a business is discussed at this point.

It may not be desirable to acquire all the assets or liabilities of a business. Some assets may not have value for the operation that the new owners intend. Some, for example, may be obsolete or may be ancillary to the business. It is also common for small business owners to have the business possess items that have little business value, but are desired by the owner. Examples of such assets are light airplanes, boats, country club memberships, and hunting or fishing properties. Similarly, some liabilities may have no business purpose, but exist for reasons personal to the owner.

Assets are categorized into two classes: tangible and intangible. Tangible assets are things that can be touched or seen, things with physical reality, such as land, buildings, and machinery. Intangibles are assets that have value, but no physical reality, such as patent rights, copyrights, trade names, and contractual provisions.

Tangible Assets

Classes of tangible assets that may be included in the purchase of a business include cash, accounts receivable, inventory, vehicles, and such property as land and buildings.

Cash. It is not normal to pay cash to acquire cash, so many acquisitions exclude cash. Be aware, however, that cash shortages are often key causes of business failure. Careful planning of the opening cash balance may require that the business's cash on hand and in banks is to be left in place. When a business operated as a corporation is purchased by acquiring all—or a majority of—outstanding stock, cash belongs to the corporation, not to the stockholders, and is included in the purchase.

Accounts Receivable. These trade debts are unpaid invoices that may not all be collectible in the short term. To investigate these, sort the list by due date and investigate the older unpaid invoices. Two common reasons for unpaid invoices are customer cash problems and disputed invoices. Collections in either situation may necessitate extensive legal or collection fees.

The buyer of a business should consider not buying any problematic accounts receivable. The price of any such accounts that *are* part of the purchase should be subject to collection: If the accounts receivable is not collected, the price of the business is reduced by the amount not collected.

Inventory. The key concern in investigating business inventory is its value at the date of acquiring the business. Many business owners never throw anything away under the belief that it might be useful someday. Operating under that theory, an owner accumulates purported "inventory" that takes up space and ties up cash.

This was the case with Automatic Door Specialists. Niemann wrote that the former owner "had stuff stashed everywhere, including his bathroom. Equally true to his reputation, he thought even piles of junk had dollar signs attached" (1990, p. 37). After much difficult negotiation over value, Niemann and the former owner finally reached an agreement completely satisfactory to neither. "When the inventory was complete, it came in at 60% of its stated value on the balance sheet and $16,000 less than my accountant's worst-case scenario" (1990, p. 38).

A reasonable approach to considering inventory is to estimate the lowest amount of inventory needed to operate the business and assume everything else is surplus with limited value.

A physical inspection of the inventory may provide clues as to its use in the business. Layers of dust may indicate lack of future use in the business, as would old delivery papers and damage incurred while in storage. Style and technological obsolescence must also be considered during the physical inspection.

Items that are the height of fashion one year may be unsaleable scrap the next. It seems that bell-bottom pants are in and out of style for a few weeks every few years. This can create a problem with inventory. Are the bell-bottom pants in the warehouse saleable inventory or are they trash that must be discarded? Clothing is not the only merchandise subject to obsolescence due to changes in style. One would be hard pressed today to sell avocado green appliances or harvest gold shag carpeting. Only a few years ago these were popular styles that were in high demand.

Technology, too, can change very rapidly, almost overnight. It is often impossible to recoup the cost of technologically obsolete inventory. Can you imagine having a large supply of typewriters when computers and printers are taking over? Or how about a computer wholesaler sitting with thousands of 486 personal computers when the Pentium computers were introduced? Both situations occurred within the last few years. IBM, Smith Corona, Olympia, and Olivetti all incurred millions of dollars of write-downs on typewriter inventories as the desktop computer took over word processing. Similarly, Compaq, IBM, Packard Bell, and numerous other computer manufacturers incurred significant losses on 386 and 486 computers when the Pentium processor was introduced.

Vehicles. Could a business owner's personal car be carried on the balance sheet of the company? How about the cars of the owner's spouse, children, and mother? While the accounting for these items might be questionable, the ability to separate out unrelated non-business assets is central to the understanding of a business.

Land and Buildings. Buildings are large assets that may be a drag on the cash flow of the business. They are usually not quickly divisible into smaller spaces or quickly expandable to meet changing business requirements. Buildings can provide tax shelters for the owners of the business and are therefore often held outside of the business to limit the number of assets exposed to a lawsuit against the corporation. A prospective buyer of a business must consider several things about buildings.

A prospective buyer must determine who currently owns any buildings. Is it the business, the current business owner, or another related owner, including the current business owner's relatives?

If buildings are not owned by the business, how many years are left on the lease? This can be a very sensitive issue. Long leases are desirable for business operations, but often are as onerous as bank financing, inasmuch as long-term leases often require personal guarantees. Buyers who take over a lease as part of the acquisition of a business are often required to make such personal guarantees. Furthermore, a long-term lease requires payments for many years, whether the business is profitable or not.

A prospective buyer should also question how the use of a building is best acquired. A short-term lease carries the least financing risk, but highest operating risk: The building could be sold or a tenant more desirable to the building's owner could sign a lease, requiring that the business be moved at the end of the lease period. A purchase ties up capital that may be needed to operate the business. A long-term lease may require relatively little cash up front, but carries as much financial risk as a purchase.

Finally, the buyer should consider who should acquire the land and buildings. While the business itself is an obvious choice, other investors may be interested in the land and buildings. These investors would buy the land and building and lease it to the company. One or all of the acquirers of a business may be one of the partners in owning the building. This may shield the land and building from claims in liability matters.

Intangible Assets

Intangible assets represent a large proportion of the value of many businesses. Intangible assets have no physical substance. Their value stems from the privileges or rights that accrue to the owner. Examples of intangible assets are goodwill, patents, trademarks, copyright, and franchises. Valuation of these items is extensively discussed in Chapter 11. What follows is a discussion of particular intangibles a potential buyer should consider.

Patents. Patents give the owner the exclusive right to manufacture, sell, and use a patented item or process for 17 years. Patents are granted to encourage the invention of new mechanical devices and processes. Although the balance sheet does show the cost paid for externally acquired patents, the value of internally developed patents is not found there. Patents can be a valuable business asset, but their value within the business is influenced by many things, including the years remaining on the patents from the 17 originally granted; the demand for the underlying item or process (patents on obsolete technologies are usually worthless); and the ability to defend a patent from cloned products. For example, sometimes the change of a single screw in a mechanical device is sufficient to declare the clone a different item from the patented one. If this occurs the value of the original patent is significantly diminished.

Copyrights. Copyrights give the owner the exclusive right to publish and sell a musical, literary, or artistic work during the life of that composer, author, or artist and for 50 years thereafter. The value of a copyright to a business is affected much as patents are.

Trademarks and Trade Names. The unique symbols or brand names that companies use in marketing products are called trademarks and trade names. Ownership is usually established by registering the trademark or trade name with the U.S. Patent Office. The business value of a trademark or trade name is a function of its recognition by candidate buyers of the product, the appropriateness of the image portrayed by the trademark or trade name to the business, and the value of trademarks and trade names in selling the type of item represented by the name. Active use of the trademark or trade name enhances its value because advertising and sales of the product improve name recognition. Dormant trademarks often have limited value.

Trade Secrets. Trade Secrets are formulas, processes, or other information proprietary to the business. Trade secrets can be of great value, as is the case of the formulas for Coca-Cola and Kentucky Fried Chicken, or of General Electric's process for cheaply manufacturing gem quality diamonds. The value of Coke and KFC's secret formulas exist because of the difficulty of exactly duplicating the products without the formula. The value of General Electric's process exists because the De Beers diamond cartel was willing to pay millions of dollars to purchase and suppress the process to maintain the price of diamonds as gemstones. When attempting to access the value of a trade secret one must consider the competitive advantage provided by the secret, the difficulty of duplicating the secret, and the likelihood of the secret being rendered obsolete. As with any other intangible asset, rights to trade secrets are freely transferable. However, once a trade secret is revealed, its use by other businesses cannot be blocked, as is the case with patents, trademarks, and trade names.

Customer Lists. Lists of customers can be very valuable assets because such lists can be used to obtain future sales. Some businesses, for example publishers, rent or sell their customer lists to other businesses. A customer list that can be sorted by geographic and other demographic attributes may add to the value of the list, because this enhances its use in targeting advertising.

A Covenant Not to Compete. The seller of a business usually signs an agreement promising not to compete with the business being sold for a reasonable amount of time and within a reasonable geographic area. *Reasonable* is an important word, because the unreasonable restraint of someone working is against public policy. Unreasonable covenants have been found to be illegal in courts. An example of an enforceable non-competition contract provision is one in which the seller of the business receives a specified number of periodic payments in return for an agreement not to compete in the same industry and geographic area as the business.

Telephone Numbers. Phone numbers with familiar names, such American Express's *1-800-THE-CARD,* or telephone numbers that have been heavily advertised should also be explicitly included in the assets to be acquired.

Liabilities

Short-Term Liabilities. Items such as accounts payable, taxes payable, and payroll payable are short-term liabilities. It is desirable to assume these liabilities and lower the offering price for the business by an assumed amount. By having cash set aside at purchase to pay these liabilities, they are more likely to be paid and the business is able to start out with a favorable credit rating. Funds for payroll and taxes payable could be placed in an escrow by the closing attorney for the purposes of prompt payment of these amounts. If a new owner does not assume these trade debts, the previous owner, who has little incentive to pay promptly, may pay these slowly, or not at all. Nonpayment may reflect negatively on the credit standing of the continuing business.

Long-Term Liabilities. Long-term liabilities often have a business asset attached as collateral. The owner of the liability, for example the bank who holds a building mortgage, has to accept the new owner of the business and possibly to relieve the former business owner of the debt. The owner of the liability often will not release the previous owner of the debt and will look to add the new owner as well. Extensive work may be needed to resolve this matter. It should be noted also that long-term leases are often treated the same as mortgages during an acquisition, and should therefore be considered as possible long-term liabilities.

Existing Lawsuits. Lawsuits for product liability claims or other matters may exist. Evaluating these is difficult, as a jury may be making the final determination. Given the potential cost of lawsuits, the sale of a business with such a liability is difficult to achieve through a meeting of the minds. Specifically excluding these lawsuits by structuring the sale of the business as a transfer of assets may be the best approach for a potential buyer.

Working Capital Adjustments

The working capital of a business is defined as current assets (typically cash, accounts receivable, and inventory) less current liabilities (typically accounts payable, accruals, taxes and wages, and salaries payable). Working capital goes up and down each day as a result of business transactions. How can a business item such as this be purchased when its value changes every day? Buyers and sellers of a business assume a certain amount of working capital exists when a deal is made to sell the business. When the business is actually sold, a physical inventory is completed and valuations of the items constituting working capital are made. A selling price adjustment to the value of the business is then made. It is much like buying or selling a used car, where one assumes that the car will have a half a tank of gas on the date of ultimate sale. If the tank is not half full, then a price adjustment is made in the selling price of the car. Assume, for example, that the car had an extra two gallons of gas on the date of the sale. If gas is \$1.75 per gallon, the seller is due an extra \$3.50 from the buyer of the car. In sales of automobiles, this amount is small in relation to the price of the car and generally is ignored in practice. For sales of businesses, the number can be quite large and, although difficult to determine, significant to the determination of a final purchase price.

This approach assumes that the inventory and other assets are to be valued twice: once at the time the deal is made, and once at the time the deal is closed. Disagreement over inventory values is very common. Buyers should become familiar with the inventory before the sale of the business is closed, as later revisions are unlikely unless a lawsuit is brought.

SUGGESTED READINGS

Baye, M. R. (1997). *Managerial economics and business strategy.* Chicago: Irwin.

Bernhard, B. D. (1997). *Selecting the right form of business: The comprehensive decision-making guide for the business advisor.* Chicago: Irwin.

The Best of INC. *guide to business strategy.* (1988). New York: Prentice Hall.

Davies, A. (1995). *The strategic role of marketing: Understanding why marketing should be central to your business strategy.* New York: McGraw-Hill.

Gilad, B., & Herring, J. P. (Eds.). (1996). *The art and science of business intelligence analysis.* Greenwich, CT: JAI.

Peters, T. J., & Waterman, R. H. (1984). *In search of excellence: Lessons from America's best-run companies.* New York: Harper & Row.

3 Defining the Product

In the early 1990s, IBM, Apple, and Microsoft were locked in a fierce competition to dominate the market for operating systems for desktop computers, a competition that would largely determine the companies' futures. IBM was attempting to leverage its name recognition as "Big Blue" and its superior market share to establish its proprietary operating system, OS2, as a replacement for Microsoft's aging MS DOS. Apple was building upon the technical superiority of the Macintosh II's processor and operating system to protect its product position as the preferred computer for education, publishing, and graphics-intensive applications. Microsoft was desperately defending its position as the primary provider of operating systems by cooperating with IBM as a junior development partner, by copying the easy-to-use features of the Macintosh into the new Windows graphic-based user interface, and by developing an integrated graphics-based operating system—the now ubiquitous Windows 95.

Today, OS2, although available, is used only on a tiny minority of computer installations. As of 1996, IBM no longer had a dominant market share of desktop computers, and in fact was a poor third to Compaq and Packard Bell (McGarvey, 1996). Apple's belated attempt to license the Macintosh operating system has been largely unsuccessful, and in 1996 Apple's share of the global market for computers had slipped to less than 7% (Swartz, 1996). Microsoft, on the other hand, despite never having sold desktop computers, has captured 95% of the market for operating systems and 75% of the market for word processors and spreadsheets.

Microsoft's dominant position today is in large part the result of the manner in which the company defined its product. As John Murdoch

(1998) explained, Microsoft defined its product as a *license* to install and distribute its flagship products, Windows 3.1, Office, and Windows 95.

> Bill Gates and Microsoft have long understood that the key to profits in the software business lies in selling licenses—not boxes. Understanding the true nature of the business has helped Microsoft achieve profit margins that drug dealers would envy. (p. 136)

IBM and Apple both continued to produce computers, seemingly unaware of their increasing dependence on Microsoft: IBM on Windows 95 and Apple on Microsoft Office for the Macintosh. Meanwhile, Microsoft withdrew from the OS2 project. The company provided identical versions of the Windows 95 operating system to every manufacturer of desktop computers, essentially negating IBM's efforts to differentiate its computers from any others. As Windows 95 became ever more prevalent and the release date of the long-promised upgrade to Office for the Macintosh became later and later, Apple's market share continued to decline.

As illustrated by the Microsoft example, product definition is essential to business success. Apple is not the only firm that has failed to dominate a market despite offering technologically superior products. Quite often, management defines the firm's product in an ad hoc manner thus losing the advantage that technical superiority can provide. Studies of both successful and unsuccessful new product projects have identified that appropriate product definition is indispensable for success (Cooper, 1994a, 1994b).

Although it seems obvious what constitutes the product of a business, quite often the *true* product is overlooked in the press of day-to-day business. The pressures of production, scheduling, financing, and cash management leave little time for the owner-manager of an entrepreneurial firm to ponder strategic product issues. In such an environment, getting the product out of the door seems much more critical than philosophical considerations of what the product really is. It is upon this rock of product definition that the launch of many an entrepreneurial venture has foundered.

THE STRATEGIC DEFINITION OF A PRODUCT

The manner is which the product of a firm is defined is an essential part of establishing an effective business strategy. Simply put, to ensure success, the product or service must meet a consumer need. Levitt (1986) first discussed the basic error of defining a product based upon function and not upon customer need.

Care must be given to defining the product. If a product is defined too narrowly, the firm risks failure because of technological obsolescence, market changes, and competitive innovations. Smith Corona, for example, defined its product primarily as typewriters. Faced with falling demand for typewriters, the company attempted, unsuccessfully, to reorganize under Chapter 11 of the Bankruptcy Code (Currid, 1995). On the other hand, Brother, Inc., which produced very similar typewriters, defined its product as *document production,* and today holds a strong position in computer printers, fax machines, and copiers (Coates, 1995).

Although the product must not be defined too narrowly, it also must not be defined too broadly. No firm can be all things to all customers. Failing to be specific in the definition of the firm's product contributes to a lack of strategic focus: The firm risks losing its way. Examples abound of the loss of strategic focus because a firm too broadly defined its product. In the 1970s, for example, many airlines defined their product as *travel services,* subsequently losing millions of dollars in ill-conceived ventures into hotels, restaurants, and tour providers, while abandoning core businesses. This provided opportunity for start-up firms, such as Federal Express, and for established firms, such as United Parcel Service, to expand into what had originally been the exclusive business of the airlines. Similarly, Eastman Kodak defined its product as *image production* and IBM defined its product as *business machines.* As a result, both firms made unsuccessful attempts to compete with Xerox and Canon in the office copier business. The list of examples of product being too broadly defined is nearly endless.

OPERATIONAL DEFINITION OF PRODUCT

A product is a combination of properties that are valuable to customers. The characteristics of a successful product include a combination of tangible and intangible attributes:

> A product may be an idea, a physical entity (a good), or a service, or any combination of the three. It exists for the purpose of exchange in the satisfaction of individual and organizational objectives. (Bennett, 1988, p. 153)

In defining the product of a firm, one must understand all three defining elements: the *idea* that the product represents to the customer, the *physical entity* that constitutes the tangible product, and the bundle of *service* that makes the product distinctive from competitive offerings.

The customers' idea of a product is often quite distinct from both the physical entity and the accompanying service. As Charles Revson is alleged to have said of Revlon products, "In the factory we make cosmetics. In the drugstore we sell hope." Success or failure is determined by the customers' idea of the product, not by the elegance of design, the quality of production, or the efficiency of distribution.

The physical reality of the product is the easy part of product definition: Most products have specific, tangible attributes that can be quantified. For example, a Merlin bicycle is made of a specific titanium alloy. The bicycle has measurable dimensions, including stand-over height, weight, and specific components for shifters. The bicycle may be matte finished, polished, or painted in a variety of colors. The price is established to position the bicycle as a luxury good, intended for serious cyclists who value high technology. Similarly, the physical reality of Starbucks' coffee, of the McDonald's Big Mac, of Carnival's Caribbean cruises, of Nike's running shoes, of Chrysler's minivans, may each be described in exquisite detail, all of which can be independently verified and completely specified.

The bundle of services that complement the physical reality of the product quite often are the features that allow customers to differentiate between products. These intangibles include elements not often considered services, such as image and brand. As many business people have discovered, a hotel room ballpoint pen is quite adequate for making notes, writing letters, and signing checks. The $100 Mont Blanc ballpoint pen, then, is likely purchased for attributes other than mere utility. Few, if any, consumers can tell one butchered chicken from another, yet both Perdue and Tyson have successfully branded chickens, commanding a significant price premium over store brands. Often, items that are considered as service can also be features of the product, such as installation, instruction, training, and maintenance.

In defining a product, one must also examine the patterns of demand for the physical product and for the associated services. The demands upon financing, cash flow, and labor management may be greatly affected by seasonal, economic, or fashion cycles. An extreme example of seasonal cycles is the demand for fireworks. For all practical purposes, within the United States, all fireworks are consumed within a one-week period immediately preceding the fourth of July. To meet demand, manufacturers must produce and store a highly perishable (and somewhat dangerous) product throughout the year to meet a highly transient sales period. Some products, such as consumer electronics (e.g., TVs, stereos, and radios) are highly sensitive to both seasonal and economic conditions: The majority of sales occur in the fourth quarter, but also fluctuate directly with the strength of the overall economy. Conversely, after-market automobile items and parts tend to sell evenly throughout the year, but demand varies inversely to the overall economy: Demand for auto parts increases during recessions. Similar, but not so extreme, patterns exist for sporting goods, apparel, small appliances, building materials, and farming and construction equipment.

Finally, the sensitivity of the market to interruptions in availability must be included in product definition. One must consider whether the product is a mass market, "impulse" item for which demand must be immediately met, as with most consumer goods, or whether the product is made only to customer order. One must also consider the availability of alternative products, the lead time of critical materials and components, and the reliability of essential suppliers.

SOURCES OF INFORMATION FOR PRODUCT DEFINITION

The most obvious source of information is the internal records of the business under consideration for purchase. Details of the physical reality of the product(s) should be maintained within the firm in the form of blueprints, engineering drawings, and specifications, and in the experience and expertise of management and production workers. The marketing department should also have current information concerning competing and substitute products. Each product should be carefully described in the strategic business plan, including details not only of the physical characteristics, but also of any essential suppliers and of any specialized raw materials and subassemblies.

Customers of the firm are the best source of information concerning the idea of the product and of the specific needs that the product fills. Those people currently buying and using the product have obviously identified a need and a use for the product, which, as discussed before, may or may not be consistent with the firm's definition of the product.

The prospective buyer should select a sample of customers. The number of customers in the sample depends in part on how many customers there are for the product: An industrial product may have very few customers, while a consumer product may have millions. A discussion of the method to determine sample size sufficient to achieve any desired level of statistic confidence is beyond the scope of this book. Any introductory statistics textbook, such as Hildebrand and Ott's *Statistical Thinking for Managers* (1998), can be consulted. For the purposes of defining the product of a small business with a large number of customers, a sample size between 45 and 90 respondents should furnish adequate results (Ricchuite, 1995). References for conducting this type of market research abound. Examples include Jarboe (1996); Shocker, Stewart, and Zahorik (1990); and Wing (1997).

The customers selected for the sample should be approached carefully, in the same manner in which a market survey is conducted. A succinct questionnaire should be developed, one that asks questions to elicit candid answers concerning the product, possible enhancements to the product, and any existing problems or disadvantages of the product. If at all possible, one should follow the questionnaire with phone calls to customers who do not return the questionnaire and with interviews of the most responsive of those who do return questionnaires. While questioning customers, one should be especially alert for unusual or unexpected uses of the product, because such responses may indicate potential new markets and improvements that may enhance the value of the product.

Competitors, too, are an indispensable source of information. One should obtain any available catalogs, product specification brochures, advertising, and promotional literature. As with the questioning of customers, be especially alert for unusual or unexpected features, uses, and services. Quite often, if approached honestly, a competitor of the business being investigated will agree to discuss business and industry issues with the potential buyer. Such discussions often produce valuable information concerning market, industry, and competitive conditions. Of course, information obtained from a competitor is likely to be somewhat biased and pessimistic, as the person already in the business is unlikely to welcome additional competition from new businesses.

The prospective buyer should also consult business organizations and associations. Most industries are represented by organizations or associations that will provide invaluable information concerning current product, market, and regulatory developments. Such information can be essential to a complete product definition. Names of industry groups may be found through library and Internet searches. For example, the International Real Estate Directory maintains a listing of associations and organizations related to real estate. The listing may be found on the World Wide Web at http://www.ired.com/dir/reassn.htm. The International Environmental Information Network maintains a list of several hundred business, industry, and professional associations and organizations, and it can be found on the web at http://www.envirobiz.com/assoc.htm. Another source of authoritative information is *Industry surveys,* which are Standard and Poor's publications carried in most major university and public libraries.

Additionally, there are many journals, magazines and newsletters specific to various businesses and industries: for example *Aviation Weekly* is directed at the aerospace industry, *Plastics World* the plastics industry, and *Oil and Gas Journal* the petroleum industry. The replacement window business has a magazine, *Fenestries.* The sign business has *Signs of the Times* and *Letterheads.* Some common businesses have multiple journals: the restaurant business, for example, is represented by *The Nation's Restaurant News, Restaurant Business, Restaurant Hospitality,* and *Restaurants & Institutions,* as well as many others. Many of these journals regularly report on industry results, developments, new products, and economic trends, all of which can be useful information in defining product.

SUGGESTED READINGS

Blaich, R., & Blaich, J. (1993). *Product design and corporate strategy: Managing the connection for competitive advantage.*New York: McGraw-Hill.

Hollins, B., & Pugh, S. (1990). *Successful product design: What to do and when.* Boston: Butterworths.

Kenkel, J. L. (1996). *Introductory statistics for management and economics.* Belmont, MA: Duxbury.

Kidder, T. (1981). *The soul of a new machine.* Boston: Little, Brown.

Mann, P. S. (1998). *Introductory statistics.* New York: John Wiley.

4 | Investigating the Market for the Product

To some degree, a market exists for any product that can be imagined: Even the prosaic buggy whip (the business school example of a stereotypically "useless" product) is currently made, distributed, and used. Horse droppings are dried, varnished and sold as *Turd Birds*; composted for use in raising mushrooms; and pulverized and bagged as fertilizer. Although the pet rock may be passé, simple stones are marketed successfully as souvenirs, paperweights, and paving material. Indeed, there is an active and extensive market for stone: The production of rock accounts for more than half of the world's output from mining!

So, for the entrepreneur, the question is usually not whether there is a market to be met, but rather whether the market is one from which a *profit* can be made. This is a very important distinction: Although there are markets for buggy whips, horse manure, and rocks, it is unlikely that the market is such that an entrepreneur can bring new features, new services, and new applications that will provide sufficient profit opportunities to make an investment worthwhile.

ANALYZING SALES HISTORY

An entrepreneur is interested not in what the market for the firm's product is or has been, but rather in making a reasonable estimate of what the market *will be*. As we have said before, no one can foretell the future. The best that one can hope for is that previous trends can be extracted from the product's sales history, general economic conditions, and other demographic and social information. The entrepreneur then makes the best forecasts possible of the opportunities for the product.

Because of the availability of data, the first area for an entrepreneur to investigate is the sales history of the firm's product. The unit selling price of each product, by model number or by other specific identification, should be collected, quarter by quarter for at least the three most recent years, from company copies of actual sales invoices. The price then should be analyzed for trend information: Is the price trending up, trending down, or staying constant? This requires more than simply looking at the differences between periods. The price of a product may well be constant in dollars, but represent a real decrease as features are added to the product over time. A well-known example of this phenomenon is the pricing of desktop computers. In 1981, a top-of-the-line IBM PC cost about $2,500. A top-of-the-line IBM PC costs about the same amount today, nearly twenty years later. However, the 1981 computer had less than 1/1,000 of the memory, operating speed, disk storage, or utility of a current computer. In real terms, the price of desktop computers is a tiny fraction of what it was in 1981.

The invoices must also be analyzed for added, nonbilled items. For example, does the invoice show a sales promotional component, such as "free" items: cables, attachments, accessories, and the like? Are there cooperative advertising allowances included with the invoice? Have return, allowance, warranty, or payment terms changed over time? All of these items have a value in themselves. A pattern of increasing features while holding price constant is essentially the same as decreasing prices for the package of features that constitute the product.

The trends in unit sales must be analyzed in a manner similar to that used to examine sales prices. Patterns of unit sales are essential to understanding the business. Are unit sales increasing, decreasing, or remaining constant? Is there a management-induced pattern to sales? Recently, the H. J. Heinz Company announced, as part of a reorganization program, that it would cease the practice of *trade loading*, in which the company shipped massive amounts of its products at the end of each quarter in an effort to increase reported sales (Collins, 1996). Heinz is far from being the only company to engage in trade loading. Such industry giants as R. J. R. Nabisco, Procter & Gamble, Bristol-Myers Squibb, Quaker Oats, and Duracell have each, at some time, indulged in the practice

(Sellers, 1992). Obviously, an interested buyer should look for such attempts at window dressing the business in the current period, as well as for the use of trade loading as a regular management practice.

A prospective buyer should also look to see if sales are seasonal. If so, then how is manufacturing scheduled to balance both cash flow and product delivery needs? Does the firm have to manufacture the product in advance of the selling season? If so, does the firm have to warehouse the product until the selling season, or is the product shipped as made to distributors who warehouse? The requirement to produce a product in advance of seasonal selling adds an inescapable element of risk to the business, because fashion, fads, and social and regulatory restrictions can change quickly, rendering warehoused products obsolete before they can be sold and shipped.

Do sales depend upon external factors, such as another manufacturer's specific design factors? Can the features of the product be preempted by other suppliers? In 1974, a small firm obtained a patent on an easy-to-use spare tire carrier for pickup trucks. The device replaced the awkward and inconvenient factory spare tire carrier, which mounted under the bed of all then-current trucks. The new product was sold to Wal-Mart stores, and was test-marketed in a single store in southwest Missouri. If the product was successful in the test store, additional orders were to be made. In 1976, both Ford and General Motors redesigned the frames of their pickups, rendering the product obsolete. Bankruptcy of the firm soon followed. Manufacturers of all types of after-market items for automobiles and trucks, such as stereo equipment, sun roofs, pickup camper shells, and bed liners, face a market that is dependent upon design factors over which they have no control.

Another form of preemption is when features of a product are included in a competitor's offerings. An example of this is the anti-trust action against Microsoft, which alleges that Microsoft engaged in unfair competition by including the features of competitors' products in Windows 95 and 98. Although analyzing the merits of the anti-trust case is beyond the scope of this book, the possibility of such practices is certainly a threat to be considered by any potential purchaser of a business.

Buyers should also examine whether or not the success of the product is dependent on tie-in sales. A tie-in sale is the sale of a secondary item, the demand for which is derived from the sale of the primary product. A common example of tie-in sales is coffee in Dunkin' Donut stores: The stores make and sell donuts, but a majority of the morning sales of donuts include coffee, which is an extremely high-margin item for the store. Examples of other tie-in sales include software and printers sold with a new computer, check stock and forms sold with home financial management programs, batteries and holsters sold with cellular phones, and extended warranty policies sold with new and used automobiles. Tie-in sales are often more profitable per unit than are sales of the primary product; however, because the demand is derived from that for the primary product, tie-ins are usually not independent products (Hudis & Brower, 1993; Varadarajan, 1985). If the tie-in can be produced and sold independently of the primary product, what is the threat to sales of the primary product? As with products dependent upon design features of other products, can the market for the tie-in be preempted, rendering the primary product unprofitable?

The fact that a product is either a tie-in sale or is dependent upon tie-ins to be successful is not, itself, sufficient reason to rule out investment in a business. However, such dependence is a weakness that can threaten the continued success of that business. On the other hand, it is possible that a product being promoted independently can also be marketed as a tie-in. An example of an independent product also successfully marketed as a tie-in is automobile financing by credit unions. Employee credit unions often combine with automobile dealers to offer package deals that combine discount prices and financing rates, thus increasing businesses for both the automobile dealer and the credit union. Which element constitutes the tie-in, the auto sale or the auto financing, depends on which business is being considered.

RETURNS, ALLOWANCES, NONREPORTED SALES, AND BARTER TRANSACTIONS

Returned items are products that are sent back to the retailer, wholesaler, or manufacturer by the customer. The history of returned items should be carefully examined by a prospective buyer to determine the levels, causes, and patterns of returns. An inescapable fact of all manufacturing is that there is always some level of required warranty attached to a product. In the case of consumer products, this usually entails accepting some amount of product return. Products may be returned for many reasons: The product might be faulty in some manner, might have failed in use, might not meet consumer needs, or might have been rendered obsolete by competing products or changing market conditions.

A returned product usually is less valuable than it was when originally shipped. Most products are returned because of failure or obsolescence. If returned for the former reason, the product must be repaired or reworked to return it to its original value. If returned for the latter reason, market forces have rendered the product less valuable, if not worthless. Regardless of the value of the product, the company incurs additional costs in the handling and remarketing of returned products: The returns must be handled and warehoused; shipping costs are incurred; records must be updated; often, returns must be reworked and repackaged; and additional sales effort must be made to dispose of the returns (van der Laan & Dekker, 1996).

The question for management is what to do with returned products. In some cases, the product may be completely marketable, needing only to be reshipped to a willing buyer. In most cases, however, a returned product is in some manner a below-quality product. Management has three options: (1) salvage or trash the product, (2) rework the product to return it to marketable quality, or (3) sell it to a firm that specializes in marketing below-quality products. Depending upon the industry, these decisions can have a major effect upon profitability and upon the image of the business. In 1995, Compaq Corporation sued Packard Bell, alleging that Packard Bell was using reworked parts in computers sold as new products. The suit led to investigations by the attorneys general of several states. After much negative publicity for both companies, a settlement was finally reached in which Packard Bell agreed to change its practices regarding the use of reworked components (Castaneda, 1996; Vijayan, 1995).

A problem similar to that of returned items is that of sales allowances. Sales allowances may take the form of reductions in the selling price from that invoiced, or may be disguised in the form of shipping extra products over the amount ordered. In many industries, allowances are conventionally used in the place of warranties in order to increase market penetration and to encourage prompt payment of invoices (Norkus & Merberg, 1994). These can be anticipated and are an appropriate part of the cost of doing business. One must be alert for nonconventional allowances: those offered because of management failure and those made for illegal or unethical purposes. Management failures that may be hidden as sales allowances include such things as late deliveries, high product failure rates, or nonspecified features (such as shipping red units when the customer ordered white ones). Illegal and unethical practices include such things as giving substantial "gifts" (or outright bribes) to buyers, billing for a low-end product and shipping a higher quality one, and providing undocumented and nonbilled services in addition to the product. These practices add to the overall cost of doing business and often hide serious business problems.

One must also be alert for evidence of nonreported sales. In many businesses, especially small owner-operated businesses and businesses in which large numbers of cash sales are made, it is common for sales to be made for cash or barter, which then are never reported for either business or tax purposes. An example of such skimming would be the owner of a pizza store accepting a $10 cash payment from a customer. The $10 is pocketed, and the sale never rung up upon the cash register. The net effect is that the owner realizes an immediate gain: The cost of the pizza is charged against those sales that are rung up, falsely reducing the reported profitability of the store, and thus reducing the tax paid.

Skimming is not restricted to small amounts or to small businesses. In 1993, Stew Leonard, chairman of Stew Leonard's Dairy Stores, and three other executives were indicted on multiple counts of tax evasion. Ultimately, Leonard pleaded guilty to tax evasion conspiracy charges in connection with the skimming of more than $17 million over a ten-year period (Ingram, 1993; "Cooked Books," 1993).

Barter practices often occur in business-to-business transactions for such things as office supplies, sign work, or maintenance done in return for goods or services. As with skimming, bartering can be used to avoid paying taxes by removing value from the company. In many businesses and in many communities, nonreported and barter transactions are a significant part of sales, and are expected by buyers and customers. The problem with the practice is that, as in the case of Stew Leonard, it is illegal and may well lead to huge fines and a prison term if detected by the IRS.

Detecting and determining the levels of product returns, allowances, nonreported sales, and barter transactions is very difficult. By design, these transactions are often deliberately kept off the records of the business. What one must do to detect them is observe the business in operation. Is there product stacked in out-of-the-way places? Is there significant reworking being done on the product? If possible, talk to those doing the reworking, shipping, and receiving: Many times, these people are themselves innocent of the questionable practices and will talk openly and freely about the amounts and timing of their work. In the case of skimming and barter, the owner of the business, in an effort to make the sale of the business more attractive, will brag about the amount of the practices and of the opportunity for a new owner to engage in the same activities.

A careful financial analysis of costs and margins, as compared to other businesses in the industry, may also provide a lead if these practices exist. However, if the practice is limited, the net effect on financial ratios may not be sufficiently large to be identified. For retail businesses, one financial record that may show nonrecorded sales and sales allowances made in the form of shipping product is the sales tax record. The gross amount of sales tax paid should reconcile with the cost of merchandise plus markup multiplied by the sales tax rate. A significant difference indicates problems. Look also for any recorded barter transactions or payments made in merchandise. Such transactions are not, themselves, illegal: It is only the nonreporting of such transactions that violates the law. The presence of these transactions in the records of the business may indicate that nonrecorded transactions have also occurred. Armed with a statement from the seller allowing disclosure, one may also obtain from local, county, and state taxing authorities the results of any completed tax audits of the business. These techniques of investigation apply equally to service businesses and to manufacturers.

DETERMINANTS OF DEMAND
FOR THE PRODUCT

No analysis of the market for a product or service is complete without a full understanding of the determinants of demand for the product or service. A determinant of demand is some underlying factor that causes sales to be made. For example, a primary determinant of demand for carpeting sales is new home sales. Similarly, one primary determinant of sales volume for mall stores is the volume of sales at the anchor stores: If sales at the anchor stores are declining, it is likely that sales of the mall stores will also decline, despite all efforts on the part of management. Once the determinants of demand are identified, they must be analyzed carefully in order to predict their future direction and the magnitude of their effect.

Identifying and understanding a market's demand determinants is neither trivial nor easy. One must both understand the industry being considered, the macro-economic forces that affect this industry, and the legislative and regulatory environment in which the industry operates. Subtle or misunderstood determinants may offer new opportunities to the business owner, as well as restrict or eliminate older ones. An example of a subtle legislative determinant is the effect of the Employee Retirement Security Act on employment. This act was intended by congress to make employee retirement plans secure against management and business failure. An unintended but important result of this act has been to add demand for temporary help. An employer does not have to offer retirement benefits to temporary workers, and thus is able to realize significant savings by maintaining full-time help at the minimum practical level.

DESCRIPTION OF THE CONSUMER

The consumer of the product or service must be well defined both psychographically and demographically. Evans and Berman (1994) define psychographics as the lifestyles, place of living, and preferences of consumers. Examples of psychographics are hobbies, vacation and recreation preferences, entertainment choices, and opinions. Demographics refer to such consumer descriptors as age, income level, gender, race, education level, number of dependents, marital status, and occupation. It is widely recognized that these factors affect demand.

Psychographic and demographic information is available from a wide variety of sources. Most large university and public libraries carry a periodical titled *American Demographics*, which publishes a variety of demographic studies and statistics. The U.S. Census Bureau maintains an Internet site at http://www.census.gov/. Additionally, over 300 CD ROMs of U.S. Census Bureau data are online at the University of California, Berkeley, and are accessible on the Internet at http://www.lib.berkeley. edu/GSSI/uc_cdrom.html. Additionally, there is at least one private company, Easy Analytic Software, Inc., that provides demographic information through the Internet at http://www.easidemographics.com. This database includes 476 separate demographic variables. Use of the database is, for the most part, free, although there are areas of the database for which an access fee is charged.

CHANNELS OF DISTRIBUTION

Also essential to understanding the market for a product or service is an understanding of the current distribution channels and selling practices. Channels of distribution are the actual, physical ways in which the product gets from manufacturer to consumer. The traditional channel of distribution is called *two-step distribution.* The manufacturer sells to a wholesaler/warehouser, who in turn sells to retailers, who then sell to consumers. Recently, many manufacturers have been attempting to shorten the distribution channel by directly marketing to the consumer. The distribution channel employed affects pricing for a product, because at each step of the distribution a markup over cost is applied to provide for profit at that level. Thus shorter distribution channels generally allow for lower retail prices.

Currently, U.S. distribution channels are undergoing significant changes. Very large retailers, such as Wal-Mart, make purchases directly from manufacturers, often demanding—and getting—special features and prices not available to other retailers. Many small manufacturers, faced with the near impossibility of gaining shelf space in the mega-stores, are resorting to direct marketing through catalogs, magazine offers, infomercials, and, increasingly, the Internet. Another important, but often overlooked, distribution channel is that of the multi-level marketer. Multi-level marketing is exemplified by the Amway Corporation. The philosophy and strategy of such marketing is exactly the opposite of the conventional strategy of shortening the distribution channel. In multi-level marketing, there are often as many as 7 to 15 levels of markup for the product. The demand for a product is built on friendships and personal contacts, rather than on competitive pricing and convenience.

Some manufacturers are using a strategic marketing technique called *pull-through marketing,* in which advertising by the manufacturer is directed at the consumer to build demand for product at the retail level. One example of pull-through marketing is the distribution of coupons by the manufacturer. Coupons represent discounts provided by the manufacturer directly to the consumer. The consumer then demands that the retailer stock the product, providing sales for the manufacturer. The more traditional marketing strategy is that of *push distribution,* in which sales are made to the retailer who then has the responsibility of building product demand.

No single distribution channel is to be preferred in all situations. Each channel has both advantages and disadvantages. The traditional two-step distribution channel provides lower levels of administrative and distribution costs for manufacturers. On the other hand, the manufacturer often becomes dependent on the warehouse-distributor, and thus loses some control over pricing, promotion, sales, and service. Certainly there are examples of successful companies that use each of the distribution channels discussed above. In the computer industry, for example, Sharp uses two-step distribution, Packard Bell sells primarily to mega-stores such as Wal-Mart and CompUSA, IBM sells directly to dealers, and Dell and Gateway both sell directly to the end user. One may also buy a computer from Amway, the archetype of multi-level marketing.

The entrepreneur who would acquire an existing business must understand the distribution channel of the business being considered. In some cases, the distribution channel provides product differentiation; in other cases, the greatest weakness of the business may well be an inappropriate or inadequate channel of distribution. In any case, a full understanding of the business can be achieved only when the issues of distribution are well specified.

THE SELLING STRATEGY

In addition to understanding the distribution channel, a prospective buyer must also explore the selling strategy. One push distribution strategy is the use of commission-based compensation. The person who makes a sale is compensated, at least in part, based on the value of the sale. In the pull-through strategy, the sales person usually receives no additional benefit in selling any specific product. For example, the check-out clerk in a grocery is paid strictly by the hour, regardless of product choices made by the consumer.

Push strategies rely largely on providing the sellers of a product with incentives to convince customers to buy that product. Pull strategies, in contrast, rely upon advertising and special promotions to convince customers to buy. Between these two extremes are all levels of mixtures, such as the auto companies that both spend millions of dollars on advertising and pay salespeople primarily by commission.

As with distribution channels, there is no single best sales strategy. All nature of products have been sold by push or pull strategies alone, as well as by various mixtures of both. In general, however, push strategies work best under three conditions: (1) The salesperson has some discretion over pricing and terms, and thus is able to make a deal with the customer; (2) the product being sold has features that clearly differentiate it from competitors; and (3) the salesperson is well trained and highly motivated. If any one of these factors is lacking, a push selling strategy is likely to fail.

MARKET RESEARCH

Defining all these market issues is a business unto itself. All accredited business schools provide degrees in the field of marketing, which concerns itself with these and other issues. Given a basic understanding of marketing, a potential buyer can access a plethora of market information. One may find information in industry-specific journals and magazines, obtain market information from trade associations, or conduct self-generated market research.

Self-generated market research is at once the most reliable source of market information and the most expensive in terms of time. The first step to conducting such research is to identify the type of customer with which the business deals: large customers, a few of whom dominate sales, or many small customers, none of whom have any material effect upon sales. Once the type of customer has been determined, a research plan can be made.

If the company is one that has a relatively few large customers, the plan is simple: Talk to each and every customer. Ask how each customer makes purchase decisions. Discuss the customer's opinion of both what is good and what is bad about the product. Request suggestions for product and service improvement. Try to elicit from each customer candid opinions of the reputation of the business. If possible, visit at least one-third of the customers in person. Make arrangements to meet with the buyers, with the persons who receive the product, and with those who use the product. Those customers who are not visited should be called by phone at a mutually agreed upon time to ensure that sufficient time will be available to answer questions fully.

If the company has many small, "nameless" customers, the market research is more complicated. The first problem is to develop a list of customer names. This can be accomplished in various ways. If customer names and addresses are part of the business records, a random sample can be drawn to be contacted, as would be done with large customers. In the absence of such customer lists, ingenuity is required. If sales are made by credit card, a list of credit card numbers can be used to obtain, for a price, the names and addresses of the customers from the card issuer. In many cases, the current telephone hook-up used to verify charge sales will automatically return the customer name and address. If time allows, one might include coupons that require customers to fill in their names and phone numbers in order to receive a free or reduced-cost product. Or one might have customers drop their business cards into a bowl or briefcase for a giveaway drawing. Some states identify counties or communities by license plate number, and so one might also go into the parking lot and copy down license plate information. Finally, one might station someone at the entrance of the business to interview customers as they leave. Questions asked should include the following: (a) How did you hear of this business? (b) Why did you stop at this business? (c) How often do you shop here? (d) Was your shopping (buying?) experience satisfactory? (e) Will you trade here again? (f) What could be done to improve product and service?

Regardless of the approach taken to find answers to the questions discussed in this chapter, the reason for obtaining the answers is to gain an understanding of the marketing issues that will allow the prospective owner to make reasonable projections of future business conditions and activities.

SUGGESTED READINGS

Clifton, P., Nguyen, H., & Nutt, S. (1992). *Market research: Using forecasting in business.* Boston: Butterworth Heinemann.

Hopkins, C. C. (1997). *My life in advertising.* Chicago: NTC Business Books.

Hopkins, C. C. (1997). *Scientific advertising.* Chicago: NTC Business Books.

Karlof, B. (1993). *Key business concepts: A concise guide* (A. J. Gilderson, trans.). New York: Routledge.

McQuarrie, E. F. (1996). *The market research toolbox: A concise guide for beginners.* Thousand Oaks, CA: Sage.

SAS Institute. (1994). *Introduction to market research using the SAS system.* Cary, NC: Author.

5 | Investigating Product Costs of Manufactured Goods

In 1986, the managers of Maxon Systems, Inc., of Kansas City, Missouri, were horrified to discover that their factory in Korea was planning to charge more than twice as much to manufacture their product—a very high resolution graphics card for computers—as the established retail price. Orders for thousands of units had already been accepted. Disaster seemed certain.

The situation had to be remedied immediately. The president of Maxon Systems, Bob Thedford, the project engineer, Robert Haler, and an industry consultant, Richard Green (one of the authors of this book), flew to Seoul to consult with factory managers in an attempt to resolve the difference of more than $100 per unit between the American and Korean estimates of manufacturing costs. Several lengthy meetings ensued. Tempers flared, as no resolution seemed possible. Finally, the comptroller for the factory, in an attempt to convince the hardheaded Americans, presented a step-by-step explanation of the process by which products were costed in the factory.

The source of the difference was, at last, identified: the manner in which factory overhead was allocated among products. The Americans had allocated factory cost in proportion to the *number* of components that were inserted into the card. The Koreans had allocated factory cost in proportion to the *cost* of the components that were inserted. It was like a terrible "good-news, bad-news" joke: The good news was that the graphics card was based on a Cirrus Logic chip set, which minimized the number of separate components required; the bad news was that the chip

51

set cost more than the discrete components it replaced. The product would be simpler, lighter, faster, and more reliable because of the use of large-scale integrated electronic chips. But because fixed factory costs were allocated in proportion to cost of the chip set, the product would be too expensive to sell!

Identifying the cause of the difference did not, however, solve the problem. Strong arguments were made in support of each allocation system. The arguments were decidedly nontrivial. The Korean factory was highly automated. All products were assembled by robotic machinery that required very little direct hand labor in the manufacturing process. The factory cost hundreds of millions of dollars and was limited in capacity. Deciding to make one product, by necessity, required that another could not be made. However, the allocation of the fixed factory cost to a specific product not only determined factory profits, but could easily determine the success or failure of that product in the market.

It is essential in any manufacturing concern to understand completely the costs of making a product. Product costs include the obvious, for example the materials from which the product is made, and the less obvious, those things that are necessary for the operation of manufacturing process, but that cannot be directly traced to any specific product. Some product costs vary directly with production levels; others are unaffected by the level of production. A clear understanding of all costs, and of the effect of varying production on costs, is required in an exercise of due diligence.

So, how did Maxon resolve the cost dispute? After much discussion, argument, and arm-twisting, a compromise was reached. The *time* that the VGA card would require for setup, production, and inspection was carefully estimated. Factory costs were allocated to the entire production run, in proportion to production time divided by the total available factory time. Maxon Systems then divided the allocated factory costs by the number of units produced to arrive at a cost per unit that could be used to calculate margins. As with most compromises, no one was completely satisfied. The Korean factory was receiving less than management desired. The American sales unit was paying more.

COSTED BILL OF MATERIAL

An investigation of product cost begins with the careful examination of the bill of material for each product being manufactured. The bill of material is a list of all materials, parts, and components used in making the product. The bill of material can be independently confirmed by comparing it to the finished product. Prices of each element can be verified by examining catalogs, calling suppliers, and interviewing sales people. Once each individual element of the bill of material has been priced, an extension can be made to determine the cost of the materials of the product.

An important consideration of costing the bill of materials is to understand the scrap and failure rates. Not every bit of material, not every part purchased, actually ends up in the product. Some material is lost in cutting, shaping, and finishing. Some parts purchased are defective when received. Scrap is an unavoidable part of the cost of making a product. The product cannot be fully costed unless appropriate estimates of the cost of scrap are included. It is usually not necessary to cost every item in the bill of materials fully: Only a few materials and components are responsible for most of the product cost. A statistical approach can be taken, determining the price of the most expensive materials and components, and also of an appropriate random sample of less costly materials and components. An often-followed rule of thumb is to confirm individually the price and consumption of the materials and components that make up 80% of the cost of the product, and to use random sampling for the rest (Posner, Brokaw, & Brown, 1990).

VOLUME EFFECTS ON COSTS

Another consideration is the price of materials and components relative to purchase volume. Generally, the larger a purchase, the lower the unit price. Purchase price is only part of the component cost, however. The cost also includes (a) the wages of the employees who make and record purchases and receipt of orders, (b) the cost of safeguarding the materials to prevent theft and wastage, (c) the interest on the money spent to make purchases, and (d) even the *opportunity cost* of not being able to use the purchase money for alternative investments while the materials and components are being warehoused and used.

The issues of determining optimum order quantities—often called *economic order quantity* or *EOQ*—and delivery schedules are of such complexity that they constitute entire courses of study in themselves. Introductory texts that may be helpful include Hesse and Woolsey

(1980), Fabrycky, Ghare, and Torgersen (1984), and Keys (1991). Additionally, most introductory textbooks in managerial accounting or financial management include brief introductions to determining optimum order quantities and to solving scheduling problems.

LABOR REQUIREMENTS

An analysis of the labor requirements to produce the product is a difficult part of product costing. Many small businesses have no objective, quantified analysis of the labor required to produce any product. A common approach for many small products is simply to estimate the time that is required to complete a batch run of the product and to apply some predetermined labor rate to that time. Often, the only way to obtain reliable statistics is to observe the product being made and time the various operations required.

The labor rate must also be examined. The cost of labor is much greater—anywhere from 25% to 60% greater—than the wage paid to the employee. There are added costs required by law, including social security and Medicare/Medicaid taxes, unemployment security insurance, and the costs of calculating, collecting, and paying income and employment taxes. Many firms also have added labor rate costs caused by paid vacations and such employment benefits as health and medical insurance and retirement plans. All of these elements, if present, must be calculated to obtain the true cost of production labor.

PRODUCTION OVERHEAD

Production overhead is always the most difficult part of product costing. Production overhead includes all the costs of producing the product that cannot be traced directly to the product, together with such items as (a) rent and insurance on the factory building, (b) wear and tear on production machinery, (c) inspection and quality control, (d) engineering changes, (e) batch setups, (f) heating and lighting, and (g) security for the plant and for employee parking areas.

The allocation of overhead to a product is, by necessity, done by estimate and it is always problematic. Traditionally, overhead costs were assumed to vary to some extent with the amount of labor performed, and overhead costs were allocated among products proportional to the amount of production labor used to make the various products. In today's manufacturing environment where overhead cost often exceeds labor cost by orders of magnitude, allocating costs to a product in proportion to labor often leads to significant miscosting of individual products. A relatively new method of allocating overhead costs is called *activity-based costing* or *ABC*. This approach attempts to identify the various activities that cause or drive costs. An example is the allocation of an engineering department. Traditionally, some amount of the cost of the engineering department would be allocated to the product in proportion to labor. Under activity-based costing, a different allocation method is chosen, often the number of change orders that are processed by the engineering department. Each unit of product is then allocated some amount of the cost of the engineering department proportional to the number of engineering change orders that the production of that particular product engenders. It is important to observe that the total amount of overhead cost is not affected by the allocation method used: Only the relative amount assigned to individual products changes. A growing body of evidence suggests that the activity-based allocation of overhead can lead to better marketing, pricing, and production decisions. ABC, however, is expensive and difficult to put into place and is, therefore, probably not practical to use as an analytical tool in performing due diligence. (See Briers, Luckett, & Chow, 1997; Landry, Wood, & Lindquist, 1997; Kaplan, 1990.)

FIXED AND VARIABLE COSTS

The best approach to estimating costs when investigating for a merger or acquisition is to disregard all allocations of overhead to the product. In the short run, overhead costs do not change in proportion to production, but are *fixed*. For example, rent is usually set by a lease contract, without regard to production level. Increasing or decreasing production will not change the cost of rent before the lease contract is up. The same is true of most overhead items. Thus, for the purposes of investigating a merger or acquisition candidate, a much easier and more objective measure is the contribution margin of each product: that is, the amount that the sales price of the product exceeds its cost of materials, parts, components, and production labor. The disadvantage to using the contribution margin for the investigation is that it explicitly assumes that all overhead is indeed fixed and will not change in response to changes in output. Certainly this assumption is not true. Overhead can, and usually does, vary to some extent with output (see Shim & Sudit, 1995).

An essential question to answer during the process of due diligence is how, when, and how much overhead costs will change when production changes. As with overhead allocation, this question cannot be answered with certainty. Any answer will be only as good as the assumptions, measurements, and estimates on which it is based. One method that may be used to determine an answer within a fixed range of production is called *account analysis.* In this process, a regression analysis between historical overhead costs, as determined from the accounts of the firm, and measured levels of production is performed. The regression assumes that there is both a fixed and a variable element to overhead costs. Using a regression technique, usually either an ordinary least squares linear regression or a multiple linear regression, an estimate of the amount of fixed cost and of the variable cost per unit may be obtained. These estimates should produce reasonably accurate estimates of overhead cost at any level of output between the minimum level and the maximum level reported in the firm's accounts. Detailed discussions of account analysis and other estimation techniques may be found in any current edition of a managerial accounting textbook. Let us, however, walk you through a sample account analysis.

Suppose that the business being considered for acquisition makes a single retail product: a special purpose desktop computer. During the exercise of due diligence, the accounts of the company are examined to determine the fixed overhead costs, including building lease, electricity, gas, water, depreciation, maintenance, cleaning, and so on. This perusal of the company records discloses the number of computers produced and the overhead costs for each month of the preceding year (see Table 5.1).

These data may be analyzed as constituting a fixed cost independent of production level and a variable cost that is a function of the number of computers produced. Thus the total cost equals the fixed cost plus the variable cost times the number of units produced. In an ordinary least squares regression this is represented as $Y = a + bX$, where Y is the total cost, a is the fixed cost, b is the variable cost per unit, and X is the number

Table 5.1   A Simple Account Analysis

Month	Computers Produced (X)	Overhead Costs (Y)	(X × Y)	X^2
January	900	$3,000	$2,700,000	810,000
February	800	2,500	2,000,000	640,000
March	900	2,900	2,610,000	810,000
April	1,000	2,900	2,900,000	1,000,000
May	1,200	3,600	4,320,000	1,440,000
June	1,300	3,400	4,420,000	1,690,000
July	1,100	3,200	3,520,000	1,210,000
August	1,100	3,300	3,630,000	1,210,000
September	1,000	3,000	3,000,000	1,000,000
October	800	2,600	2,080,000	640,000
November	700	2,300	1,610,000	490,000
December	800	2,600	2,080,000	640,000
Summation	11,600	$35,300	$34,870,000	11,580,000

SOURCE: Adapted from Garrison (1985).

of units made. These variables may be estimated by simultaneously solving two equations:

$$\Sigma XY = a\Sigma X + b\Sigma X^2$$

and

$$\Sigma Y = na + b\Sigma X.$$

Solving these equations reveals that the fixed costs equal $973.18 and variable costs are $2.36 per computer built.

Suppose that planned production is 10,500 units for the month immediately following acquisition. The projected overhead cost is

$$Y = \$973 + (\$2.36 \times 10,500 \text{ computers}),$$

or $25,753. The overhead cost per computer, then, is $25,753 ÷ 10,500, or $2.47. Overhead costs may be estimated for this data set for any level of production between a minimum of 700 units and a maximum of 13,000 units.

STAFFING REQUIREMENTS

An important analysis in considering an acquisition is that of production crew size and essential skills. An investigation should be made to ascertain that crew sizes are appropriate for the production tasks and production level. Observation of the production process often reveals clues to the appropriateness of crew size. If the product is not being completed either on time or to the desired quality level, one might suspect that crew size is inadequate or that the crew members are not appropriately skilled. Conversely, if product is invariably produced on time and to standard, but workers seem to be standing around doing little, crew size may be excessive or workers may be being assigned tasks too simple for their skill level. Both situations are undesirable in that each leads to excessive costs. If time allows, the most rigorous approach to this analysis is to complete a classical time and motion study of the manufacturing process.

If inappropriate crew size or skill levels are detected, a further analysis is needed to determine the causes. Often, production workers are unionized and collective bargaining agreements restrict management's ability to assign workers to appropriate crews or according to individual skills. Within a certain class of job, most union agreements require that assignments be made based on seniority. There may also be elements of the production process that require a large crew for relatively short periods within the process, causing slack at other times. It may be that the sales of the business do not support production at a more efficient level. A minimum size crew may be required to complete the production process; however, the same crew could produce more within any given shift if the work were available. Because there is a minimum crew size, employment cannot efficiently be changed by less than the count of a full crew.

An example of crew-determined staffing is found in flight departments. Most turbojet aircraft require crews of two or three persons: a captain, a first officer (copilot), and, for some aircraft such as a Boeing 727, a flight engineer. Because of specific license and experience requirements, persons filling these jobs are not necessarily interchangeable. Thus an expansion of the flight department may well require hiring not just one additional pilot, but an additional crew of pilots.

A final consideration for production staffing is the issue of key persons. As can be true in any area of a business, it is not uncommon in small businesses for individual workers to be irreplaceable because of unique skills or experience. It is also true that some workers, in order to enhance job security, deliberately refuse to train coworkers in essential skills. If such *key persons* exist in the business being acquired, the success of the business could be threatened if these workers were to sever employment for any reason. Thus it is important to identify any key persons during the due diligence process.

Although there is no one sure way to determine if any specific worker is a key person, the problem can be approached by simultaneously using several methods. First, one should simply ask the current owners, management, and workers if any key person exists. The question might be phrased in different ways and asked several times: Is there anyone whom you would hate to have quit? Who is the best worker on the line? Who has been here the longest? Why has he/she stayed so long? If you run into a problem you can't solve, to whom do you go for help?

Second, during the physical inspections made of the plant, one should be alert for signs of key persons: workers who are treated with deference, workers who control their workspace, or workers who determine their own work times and tasks. Third, one should carefully consider any tasks that require high skills, such as welding exotic metals; blowing or forming glass; erecting tall steel structures; manufacturing, installing and maintaining fiber-optic systems; or performing critical laboratory tasks. Fourth, consider any jobs within the business that require advanced education, such as medical doctors, research scientists, computer programmers, or graduate engineers. Although such highly educated people may not be key persons inasmuch as their knowledge, skills, or experience is unique, it is quite possible that hiring a replacement may be difficult, expensive, and time-consuming.

PRODUCTION EQUIPMENT

The nature and quantity of production equipment required is determined both by the predicted highest level of production within a year and by the capacity of the equipment. Few businesses are able to sell and produce evenly throughout the year. Because of seasonal effects, macroeconomic factors, required maintenance on equipment, and restrictions on labor and materials availability, most manufacturing firms plan for varying levels of output throughout the year. It is necessary that there be sufficient production equipment capacity to meet the highest forecast output level, with an excess margin of capacity, depending on the reliability of the machinery.

Equipment does not function 100% of the time. No matter how carefully used or how well maintained, machinery breaks. It needs sometimes to be removed from the production process for the purpose of maintenance. These downtimes have the effect of reducing the amount of production machinery available. The amount of downtime varies with the nature of the equipment and the nature of its use. Solid state control units may function for thousands of hours with no maintenance of any nature. Cranes and hoists require daily maintenance, and are examined for fluid servicing and systems functions before and at the end of each work shift. Heavily used cutting, milling, and shaping machines may require maintenance throughout the production cycle. Whatever the specific needs of the production equipment, adequate downtime must be put into the production schedule to perform required maintenance.

A critical consideration with existing production equipment is its age, condition, and state of obsolescence. The age of the equipment should be apparent from the business's accounting records. If for some reason the age cannot be determined from the records, identification plates on the machinery should provide information: model and serial numbers, for example, would allow the age to be determined either from the original maker of the machinery or from trade sources, such as *Blue Book* publications. Condition can be estimated by first examining the equipment carefully, then collating the maintenance and repair costs from the account records, and finally questioning the operators of the equipment about breakdowns and maintenance times. The state of obsolescence can be determined only by someone who is truly expert in the industry. Such expertise can be found in salespeople who represent the particular type of machinery in question, in engineers who are active in the industry, and in consultants to the industry and to other businesses in the industry.

PRODUCTION LAYOUT ANALYSIS

Within each manufacturing plant, there is a layout of the location of production equipment and work stations. This layout needs to be drawn on paper or entered into a computer program, and the flow of materials, product, and workers through the facility should be analyzed for efficiency and safety. Most large manufacturers have computerized or blueprint layouts, and are constantly making efforts to improve efficiency. Few small manufacturers have even considered such issues, being restrained by space and capital (Francis, McGinnis, & White, 1992).

SCRAP AND BY-PRODUCTS

A final element of product costs to analyze is the scrap and by-products of the production process. Some scrap has significant value of itself. For example, a photograph processing shop that develops significant amounts of black-and-white film also produces silver as a scrap product. There is a ready market for silver, and the metal is valuable of itself. More often, however, the scrap has so little value that it cannot be sold, and in fact significant cost must be incurred to dispose of it. Examples of such scrap include used motor oil, batteries, used tires, and various hazardous chemicals employed in the production process. Disposing of all of these items imposes significant costs on the business, both for the physical disposal and for the recordkeeping required by the Environmental Protection Agency.

VOLUME ANALYSIS

Volume analysis is the process by which the effect of different levels of output on product costs is estimated. Such an analysis is relatively simple to complete using modern computer programs, although some programming skills are needed. A simple approach is to use a spreadsheet program. Each product is listed down the first column. Across each row, the volume of each product, the price at which the product can be sold, and the variable costs of materials and production labor are entered. The total contribution margin of each product is calculated by netting price against variable costs, and then multiplying the resulting number by planned production volume. The sum of the contribution margins of all products to be produced is netted against the total fixed costs of the business, including corporate, sales, and administrative and manufacturing

Table 5.2   A Simple Volume Analysis

Product	Volume (v)	Sales Price (p)	Variable Costs (c)	Contribution Margin $(m = (p - c) \times v)$	Fixed Costs (f)	Profit/Loss $(m - f)$
Window sign	1,500	100	55	67,500		
Wall sign	750	500	400	75,000		
Pylon sign	500	1,000	800	100,000		
Sum of contribution margin				242,500		
Total corporate fixed costs and profit/loss					250,000	− 7,500

overhead costs. The net amount is the predicted profit (or loss) at the forecast production level for each product.

For example, suppose that a business produces three products: a window sign that sells for $100 wholesale; an internally illuminated location sign, which mounts directly to the building, that sells for $500; and a pole-mounted sign, which can be lettered with the customer's business name, that sells for $1,000. A careful analysis of the costs of the products reveals a total corporate fixed cost of $250,000 and a profit margin (or, in this case, a loss) of $7,500 (see Table 5.2).

Once set up, a volume analysis spreadsheet becomes a quick "what-if" analysis. What if the sales of one product exceed the forecast? What if the price of a product changes? Simply insert the higher volume assumption or the change in product price, and the net effect on profit is instantly calculated. What if the cost of materials or energy in our sample business increases? Suppose a special order is considered by marketing: World-Mart discounters will purchase 2,500 window signs at a price of $85 each. If management accepts the order, the sales of wall signs will drop by 350 units and the production of pylon signs will have to be reduced to 420 units. What is the effect on profits? Make the appropriate changes to variable product and overhead costs, and the effect is instantly calculated: The total corporate fixed cost is unchanged, but the business now has a profit margin of $35,750 (see Table 5.3).

As with the issues of operational research, a complete discussion of volume effects is beyond the scope of this book. Introductory discussions of volume effects may be found in any general managerial accounting

Table 5.3   "What If" Changes to the Volume Analysis

Product	Volume (v)	Sales Price (p)	Variable Costs (c)	Contribution Margin $(m = (p - c) \times v)$	Fixed Costs (f)	Profit/Loss $(m - f)$
Window sign	1,150	100	55	51,750		
Special order	2,500	85	55	75,000		
Wall sign	750	500	400	75,000		
Pylon sign	420	1,000	800	84,000		
Sum of contribution margin				285,750		
Total corporate fixed costs and profit/loss					250,000	35,750

textbook, such as Hilton (1994). More complete discussions may be found in advanced managerial accounting texts, such as Magee (1986) or McNair (1993). Additionally there are innumerable articles and scholarly studies, such as Creese (1993) and Hirsch (1993).

SUGGESTED READINGS

Cokins, G. (1996). *Activity-based cost management making it work: A manager's guide to implementing and sustaining an effective ABC system.* Chicago: Irwin.

Shank, J. K., & Govindarajan, V. (1993). *Strategic cost management: The new tool for competitive advantage.* New York: Maxwell Macmillan International.

6 | Investigating Purchased Items

One key advantage of any business is the ability to purchase items at stable prices that are low enough to allow for a large enough markup to provide business profits. Often, purchasing ability constitutes the sole competitive advantage of the business. Thus it is essential to examine closely the purchase records of the business being considered for merger or acquisition.

There are several factors to be examined when considering purchased items: the cost of the items, purchase quantities, quantity discounts, delivery, terms of purchase, return policies for defective and obsolete product, technical and training support, and the stability and reliability of key suppliers. Despite the seeming simplicity of these items, actually determining answers to purchase questions is often quite complex. Rarely can one simply open a catalog and read the details of purchasing. Suppliers can and do negotiate unique terms for individual purchasers. The terms of such agreements can be determined only by a perusal of contracts, invoices, and warranty statements.

DISCOUNTS AND PURCHASE QUANTITIES

Quantity discounts are usually made available to those purchasers who can buy in quantities greater than can be consumed by individual users. The justification for quantity purchase discounts is that the seller can realize savings in the cost of order handling, packaging, shipping, and collection by making one large sale versus making numerous smaller sales. These economies of scale can then be passed on to the purchaser in the form of reduced prices. There are at least two types of quantity discounts: spot orders and annual requirement basis. A spot order is simply a one-time large quantity order. An annual requirement basis means that a commitment to accept a large quantity is made, with the product being shipped at various times during the following year. While both arrangements for quantity purchases are common, the annual requirement basis is usually limited to authorized dealership and franchise arrangements.

Simply obtaining a lower price by ordering larger quantities is a simplistic and dangerous approach to purchasing. The cost of purchasing product is only part of the cost of a product. The full cost of a product includes delivery costs, warehousing costs, interest on borrowed money used to purchase it, opportunity cost of capital, warranty costs, and lost sales due to out-of-stock conditions, spoilage, and returns. Further complicating the understanding of purchasing costs is the fact that the costs listed above are mutually dependent: Lowering the cost per unit by making a large quantity order will increase warehousing, interest, and opportunity costs. Each firm has at least one optimum order quantity that will minimize total product costs. Optimum order quantity can be calculated only if the behavior of *all* relevant costs is fully understood. Thus the exercise of due diligence requires that the amount, timing, and behavior of all product costs be carefully examined.

Optimum Order Quantity

The optimum order quantity is also called *economic order quantity* or *reorder point.* There are three sets of costs associated with inventory: the cost of ordering inventory, the cost of carrying inventory, and the costs of having insufficient inventory on hand (see Table 6.1). The optimum amount of inventory to carry is the amount that will simultaneously minimize these three sets of costs.

As a practical matter, a minimization of these costs is difficult to achieve. For ease in understanding and computation, the problem is usually broken into two questions: First, how much inventory to order? Second, how often to place an order? The answer to the first question is called the economic order quantity; the answer to the second, the reorder point.

Economic Order Quantity. To illustrate the first, assume that a company projects its total orders for a particular subassembly to be 3,000 units annually. An examination and analysis of the accounts discloses that it costs the firm $10 to handle a purchase order and $0.80 to hold one unit in inventory. The order cost is calculated by multiplying the cost of handling purchase orders by the number of purchase orders made, or, in our example, 3,000 × $10, which produces an order cost of $30,000. The holding cost is figured by multiplying the cost of holding one unit by the average number of units in inventory. If we assume that the average number of units in inventory is one-half the number of units ordered, then in our example the holding cost is $0.80 × 1,500, or $1,200. Thus the total annual cost of inventory will be the sum of the order costs and the holding costs: $31,200.

This can be represented graphically:

Economic Order Quantity

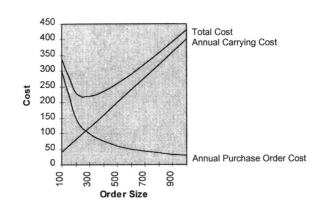

As can be seen from the graph, the minimum cost occurs where the annual purchase order cost equals the annual carrying cost. This problem can also be approached by using calculus to determine the minimum total order cost. Calculus provides the following equation:

$$O = \sqrt{\frac{2Qp}{C}}$$

Table 6.1   Costs Associated With Inventory

Costs of Ordering Inventory	*Costs of Carrying Inventory*	*Costs of Insufficient Inventory*
Clerical costs	Storage space	Customer dissatisfaction
Transportation	Handling	Erratic production
	Property taxes	Lost quantity discounts
	Insurance	Inefficient production runs
	Obsolescence	Added transportation
	Interest on capital	Lost sales
	Opportunities lost	

where O = the order size in units,
          Q = the annual quantity used in units,
          P = the cost of placing one order, and
          C = the annual cost of carrying one unit in inventory.

Solving the equation with the above data provides an economic order quantity of 274 units.

Reorder Point. The second part of the solution to the optimum order quantity is to calculate how often to place an order for the economic order quantity. The point at which to reorder depends on three factors: (1) the economic order quantity, (2) the *lead time,* or time required from placing the order to receiving the inventory, and (3) the rate of usage during the lead time.

If the rate of usage is constant, calculating the reorder point is easy: Simply multiply the lead time by average usage to arrive at the reorder point. In the example, if average usage is even, then average weekly usage equals 3,000 units ÷ 52 weeks, or 57.7 units per week. Assume that the lead time is 3 weeks and that the economic order point is 274 units. The reorder point, then, is 3 weeks × 57.7 units per week, or 173 units. Thus an order should be placed every time the inventory drops to 173 units in stock.

However, few firms can count on constant usage during the lead time or on consistent lead times. Most firms, therefore, calculate a level of *safety stock,* a surplus of inventory to meet those times of higher usage or those times when delivery of inventory is late. Using a safety stock, the reorder point becomes (lead time × average usage) + safety stock.

DELIVERY AND TERMS OF PURCHASE

Delivery may be included in the price for purchased items, paid by the seller and charged to the buyer, or paid directly by the buyer. Shipping costs may be invoiced for later payment, due on delivery, paid in part as a deposit with the remainder due at a later time, or required to be paid in full prior to the product being loaded at the point of shipment. Delivery often is a very large component in the total cost of purchased products. The amounts, timing, and manner of payment of shipping costs may have a serious effect on the cash flow and on the profitability of the purchaser. Thus a full understanding of current delivery methods and costs may disclose areas in which savings may be realized, providing a competitive advantage for an astute entrepreneur.

Sales terms are similarly variable. A product may be sold to be paid for only upon subsequent sale; this is called a consignment sale. The product may be *floor-planned*: that is, financed by the seller for a specific period of time at a predetermined interest rate. The product sale may be subject to some standard payment schedule, such as a discount of 2% if paid within 10 days of receipt and otherwise due and payable 30 days after delivery. In some cases, the seller may well demand that the product be paid for in full prior to shipment from the factory.

Items that are delivered great distances, such as imports to the United States from Pacific Rim factories, are usually sold in this last manner. Often, factories in the Pacific Rim will sell *only* complete cargo containers for either seaborne or air shipment, which must be paid in full in advance of shipment. Depending on the nature of the item being shipped, the quantity and value of a container can range from a few tens of items and thousands of dollars, as with bicycles, up to thousands of items and millions of dollars, as with computer chips and pharmaceuticals. The reseller of such items adds value by warehousing, assembling, and repackaging the items into smaller quantities, and then distributing either to retailers or to the ultimate consumer.

Many entrepreneurial enterprises operate solely in this manner: purchasing large quantities of items, repackaging them, and reselling them. One of the largest sellers of personal computers, Dell Corporation of Austin, Texas, started in exactly this manner. The company purchased various computer subcomponents and resold them, either individually as user-installed upgrades, or assembled into complete computers. The company throughout its early years had no production facilities other than for the simple assembly of purchased items. Recently, Schwinn Bicycles ceased manufacturing in the United States and now imports all of its bicycles, primarily from factories in Taiwan.

CHARACTERISTICS OF THE SUPPLIER

Once the quantity, delivery, and terms of sales of the purchased products are determined, one must consider the characteristics of key suppliers. Questions to be answered include the following: (a) Is there an exclusive purchasing agreement? (b) Does the supplier sell to enterprises that will be in competition with the business under examination? (c) What services does the vendor provide in addition to product? (d) What are the return policies of key suppliers? (e) How stable, successful, and reliable is the supplier? (f) What are the sources and reliability of labor and materials?

A key element to successful reselling is to have an enforceable *exclusive* purchase arrangement with the supplier. Such arrangements ensure the entrepreneur that the supplier cannot sell directly to the ultimate customer or to competitors. Such direct selling can be a serious threat to the profitability and ultimate success of a business. Because of the serious effect that direct selling can have on the success of distributors and resellers, it must be prevented, if possible. A few years ago, a report was circulated that IBM was going to bypass their dealers and sell computers directly to discount outlets. The IBM dealers immediately organized to bring a lawsuit: Had IBM sold directly to discounters, dealers would have been seriously damaged by having to compete with firms that have an advantage in purchasing power and overhead costs. It turned out that the report was false: IBM had not intended any such thing. Indeed, IBM took out large ads in various newspapers announcing that the rumor was false.

In many cases, key suppliers attempt to sell directly to customers, outside established dealership or franchise organizations. One example is the familiar outlet store. This has become common in the clothing business, to the distress of the management of department stores. If a customer can purchase a brand-name item from an outlet store at a price below what the department stores offer, the department store loses not only that particular sale, but also the ancillary sales that result from store traffic levels. One response of the management of department stores has been to pressure manufacturers to locate outlet stores distant from population centers. Thus one finds large outlet stores in Branson and Lake Ozark, but none in St. Louis or in Kansas City; in suburban New Jersey, but not in New York City.

One form of exclusivity is area designation for authorized dealerships. Often dealerships include a protected geographical area in which the dealer holds an exclusive right to resell the product. This provides some assurance that the consumer cannot purchase directly from the supplier. It gives a dealer some hold on consumers within the exclusive area, in that going to a competing dealer is less convenient than dealing "at home." If the business under examination is an authorized dealer or franchisee of the supplier, then the terms of the dealership or franchise must be carefully reviewed for issues of exclusivity and the ability to expand into other areas.

Dealership agreements and franchises are not necessarily transferable. Often the parent company or franchisor reserves (a) the right to purchase the business if the dealer or franchisee sells, (b) the right to *qualify* and approve any buyer of the dealership or franchise, or (c) the right to cancel the agreement if the dealer or franchisee sells. Such covenants greatly affect the value of the business being examined. Certainly the buyer of a dealership or franchise should make the purchase contract contingent on the transfer of the dealership or franchise agreement at terms favorable to the purchaser.

Exclusive arrangements are not always favorable to dealers. Exclusive sales arrangements, including dealerships, often preclude the business from purchasing from other suppliers. Also, provisions that set minimum purchase levels, pricing, or financing arrangements are commonly included in dealership contracts. In the early 1980s, authorized IBM dealers were prohibited from discounting, but were subject to strict requirements to purchase large numbers of computers. Failure to accept delivery of the required minimum number of computers would cause the loss of IBM dealership rights. This led to a widespread gray market where dealers sold IBM computers "out the back door" to resellers, who either simply discounted them or added various components, such as hard drives and internal modems, and then sold the upgraded computers as "value added units." Although the IBM dealers who engaged in gray-market selling were supplying competitors, for many the lost sales were less costly than losing dealership status would have been. Regardless of the effects on any single dealer, the existence of the gray market drove down prices for IBM computers. During the 1980s, many IBM dealers suffered business failure as a result.

Franchise arrangements can contain similar restrictions, which require the franchisee to make all purchases directly from the franchisor or from the franchisor's authorized suppliers. At one time, it was a common requirement that fast food franchisees were required to purchase soft drinks solely from either Coca-Cola or Pepsi. Even now, it is most unlikely that one will find a restaurant that offers Coca-Cola, Dr. Pepper, and 7-Up simultaneously. Such purchase requirements can be helpful by providing significant economy of scale for customized items, such as preprinted containers and advertising materials; however, they can be quite costly by preventing price shopping for commodity items, such as chicken parts, ground meats, bread items, or furniture.

Exclusivity agreements offer both advantages and disadvantages for resellers of a product. When examining a business subject to such arrangements, the implications of the agreements must be carefully considered, both for short-term profitability and long-term business success. No matter what the implications, all restrictive agreements represent a loss of control and flexibility for the business owner.

Of critical importance to all resellers is the return policies of key suppliers. A business does not want a large number of returns, either from the customer to the reseller or from the reseller to the supplier. Returns are expensive: Not only is there the direct expenses of handling and accounting, but there is an indirect cost in the loss of customer goodwill due to a perception that the merchandise is of shoddy quality.

Sometimes returns are unavoidable, however. Products do fail, fashion changes, and economic downturns may cause sales to be less than predicted for the selling season. If such events happen, the return policy of the supplier can make the difference between failure and the continued existence of the business. In some cases, suppliers do not accept returned merchandise; rather, the supplier will furnish credit for distressed, failed, or returned product that may be applied against future purchases. Often returns are accepted, but limited to specific percentages of purchases, or to merchandise returned by customers for specific reasons, such as product failure. In consumer electronics, a common return policy is that merchandise can be returned only for item-by-item replacement. In fashion goods, such as clothing and accessories, there are often no returns allowed for any reason. The merchandise is dated in that there is very little market for last season's fashions. Dresses that sell in season for hundreds or even thousands of dollars may not sell for tens of dollars next season. Some products, such as the 1970s polyester knit leisure suits for men, have no market value once the fad ends. The merchandise cannot even be given away, let alone returned to the supplier. Stores that purchased too many leisure suits encountered additional costs of trashing the outdated merchandise.

Vendors and suppliers commonly offer services in addition to the product itself. One often overlooked function of suppliers is technical and training support. One constant, costly, problem for small business owners is training employees. Vendors, especially of technologically advanced products, often offer specific training for employees of customers. Training offered may include business management issues, sales and marketing techniques, and maintenance of product. Vendors often offer store displays, product literature, promotional items, advertising support, and materials. A common vendor-offered service is cooperative advertising. Cooperative advertising can be on a national basis, as when an IBM advertisement in the *Wall Street Journal* lists authorized dealers nationwide. More commonly, however, cooperative advertising takes the form of either cash payments or credit on account to reimburse branded product advertising. Cooperative advertising usually constitutes some predetermined percentage of actual approved advertising costs, up to a limit based on the value of total purchases. Such services can be very valuable, but are rarely considered in determining the value of a business acquisition. Details of available support services and cooperative advertising can be obtained from the sales representatives of the key suppliers.

Of critical concern is the financial and business stability of key suppliers. This is especially true when an authorized dealership or franchise relationship exists between a business and its key supplier. Often there is no alternative source for critical products, other than the parent company. Failure of the key supplier will cause inescapable failure of dependent businesses.

Examples of the business failure of firms because of the key supplier's financial instability abound in the fast food business. Two such are Arthur Treacher's Fish and Chips and Minnie Pearl's Fried Chicken. In each of these businesses, the franchisor entered business in competition with an entrenched, widely known firm: Arthur Treacher's with Long John Silver's Fish 'n Chips, and Minnie Pearl's with Colonel Sanders' Kentucky Fried Chicken. In both cases, it was not the individual franchisee stores that went bankrupt: The parent franchisor business failed. Because of lack of cooperative advertising, lack of source of supplies, and loss of purchasing power, the individual stores soon ceased operation as well, resulting in substantial losses for the franchisees. Similar failures have happened in many other businesses, as well. Packard Bell was a major manufacturer of television sets. The current Packard Bell computer company purchased rights to that company's sole remaining asset: the name *Packard Bell*. Studebaker automobiles has not been in business since the mid-1960s. All Studebaker dealers either made arrangements with one of the remaining auto manufacturers or ceased business. Osborne Computers was the first manufacturer of portable computers based on the Intel 8086 chip and the Microsoft DOS operating system. The failure of Osborne caused the subsequent failure of several computer dealerships who were not able to find alternative product sources.

When considering the business stability of key suppliers, one should determine if the supplier is a wholesaler, a representative of the manufacturer, or the manufacturer itself. Such distinctions can be important. The manufacturer may well be quite successful and stable, while the wholesaler of the products is not. The converse also may be true: the wholesaler may be stable, with access to products from a variety of manufacturers, while any specific manufacturer might not be. The manufacturer may have delivery, financing, and return policies for direct buyers that are not available to those who purchase from wholesalers or from independent sales representatives. Wholesalers may not deal in the full range of products of any specific manufacturer, opening the chance that an authorized dealer may not have access to desirable products.

An example is Giant Bicycle Manufacturing Co. of Taiwan. Giant is the world's largest manufacturer of bicycles, producing bicycles under its own name, Giant, and for most well-known U.S. brands, including Schwinn, Trek, and Specialized. Giant Bicycle, Inc., although a subsidiary of the manufacturer, is solely an importer and distributor of Giant brand bicycles. In 1990, Giant Bicycle, Inc., imported a limited number of fully-equipped touring bicycles, called the *Excursion*. Although an essentially identical bicycle is popular in Europe, the bicycle failed to sell in the

United States. Giant Bicycle, Inc., did not accept returns of *Excursions* from authorized dealers. Thus some dealers, as long as three years later, in 1992, still had unsold *Excursions* in stock. The bicycles were ultimately sold at deep discounts from the retail price, often at amounts significantly below the dealer cost. Had a bike shop been somehow able to deal directly with Giant Manufacturing of Taiwan, it might have been possible to either return the *Excursions,* or to trans-ship them to Europe, where the bicycles were a successful product.

A final issue in the characteristics of key suppliers is the nature and security of the supply of raw materials and labor. As the world economy develops, there are alternate sources for every raw material. One may believe that little, short of a major war, is likely to disrupt seriously the supply of ordinary materials. However, such disruptions do occur. The oil embargoes of the 1970s not only limited the supplies of feed stocks for energy, chemicals, and plastics, but also acted to drive prices to previously unthinkable levels. Many companies, including manufacturers of light aircraft, boats, and fiber-reinforced resin products were forced from business because of their inability to obtain materials. Similarly, environmental issues may make handling available materials prohibitively expensive. Currently, no manufacturer makes mercury-filled thermometers in the United States. The glass tubing for thermometers is drawn domestically, then shipped to Brazil where it is filled with mercury. In fact, obtaining and using many materials, such as mercury, asbestos, and carbon tetrachloride, is extremely difficult and expensive, if not impossible.

The nature and supply of labor can also be a serious issue. Recently, several clothing manufacturers have found themselves the target of controversy and boycotts over the issue of child or forced labor. Importing products from countries where children and prisoners are commonly forced to work at low wages under extreme conditions has become not only ethically suspect, but also reason for organized boycotts by consumer and human rights groups. Dependence on a supplier who uses labor sources unacceptable in the United States can be cause for business failure. The political situation of supplier nations should also be considered. If the key supplier is located in an area governed by a repressive, authoritarian regime, strikes, demonstrations, and revolution may be a serious threat to continued shipments of a product.

Merely finding out the nature of a key supplier, be it manufacturer, representative, or wholesaler, is not sufficient for the purposes of due diligence. There is often wide variation among regions within a single company. For example, a bicycle wholesaler may have more than one warehouse-distribution center. The Chicago warehouse may be poorly run, often shipping incorrect product, making billing errors, missing deadlines, and so on. The Atlanta warehouse, on the other hand, may be efficient and reliable. The issue in investigating the key suppliers of a potential merger or acquisition is to find out the reliability of the suppliers with which that business deals. One way to ascertain the answer to such questions is to talk with people in the business who for product or geographical reasons are not likely to be competitors. If you are investigating a sign shop in Kansas City, talk with the owners and managers of sign shops in Indianapolis, Oklahoma City, and Dallas. Attend industry conventions and trade shows to meet and question people knowledgeable in the business. It is unimaginable that anyone would attempt to enter the consumer electronic business and not attend the summer Consumer Electronics Show in Chicago in July; or the computer business without attending a winter COMDEX in Las Vegas in November.

SUGGESTED READINGS

Monczka, R., Trent, R., & Hanfield, R. (1998). *Purchasing and supply chain management.* Cincinatti, OH: South-Western College Publishing.

Przirembel, J. L. (1997). *How to conduct supplier surveys and audits.* Palm Beach, FL: PT Publications.

Steele, P. T., & Court, B. H. (1996). *Profitable purchasing strategies: A manager's guide for improving organizational competitiveness through the skills of purchasing.* New York: McGraw-Hill.

7 | Facility Concerns

Niemann described the sight of his new building in his 1990 article:

> I pulled up in front of the offices of Automatic Door Specialists. The building was too ugly to qualify as nondescript. It was a one-story structure painted industrial tan that had obviously been a retail establishment in a former life—it had plywood where a couple of storefront windows used to be.
>
> My wife shot me a look that said, "You've *got* to be kidding!"
>
> Inside was horrifying. Piles of steel, aluminum, and wood scattered about. Some benches with tools. Shelves stacked with pieces of equipment with yellowing tags that said "bad" or "rebuilt." . . . Overhead were steel supports . . . piled high with aluminum, pipes of every shape and size, old carpet. The parts section consisted of hundreds of cubbyholes stuffed with widgets, gizmos, screws, bolts, wire, gears, and things that had been stashed there temporarily—20 years before.
>
> Yes, this was definitely a mistake. (p. 34)

Although few would-be acquirers of a business will ever find a business location in as extreme distress as did Niemann, some disappointment in the business facilities is inevitable. No business is ever in perfect facilities, and so some room for improvement is bound to be found during the exercise of due diligence.

The goal of examining the facilities of the business being considered for acquisition is to determine if the size, location, and condition of the facilities are appropriate for the business. Unnecessary costs will be incurred if the facility is either too large or too small for current or projected business volume. An inappropriate location may force relocation at great expense and business disruption. Only a fool would put a welding shop in a wooden building. One would have to be a masochist to attempt to operate a foundry near a residential area. Undesirable parts of town are, for good reasons, exactly that: *undesirable*. A dilapidated building can be the original "money pit," and may be impossible to insure at any cost. On the other hand, "dirty" businesses, such as welding shops, body repair, radiator rebuilders, and sign manufacturing, need to be in rugged buildings that will not be damaged by the inevitable fumes, spills, scrapes, and bangs that are part of the business processes.

To evaluate the capacity of facilities, it is necessary to understand the physical requirements for production and handling of the prospective business's product or service.

The appropriate size and location will be set by the interaction of several of the business's characteristics, including (a) the type of business, (e.g., manufacturing, wholesale, retail, or service), (b) the need for transportation access, (c) the nature and number of employees of the business, and (d) competing and complementary enterprises. Unfortunately, there is no simple set of rules that can be followed to evaluate the facility needs of a business. The only approach is to carefully consider all aspects of the business, both quantitative and qualitative, and to make an informed judgment.

SIZE AND CAPACITY CONCERNS

The initial process of determining the appropriate size of facilities begins with the time and layout studies discussed in Chapter 5. Depending on the type of business, there are several starting points for this analysis. Manufacturing firms must be concerned first with actual area needed for production. Wholesalers must have adequate space for warehousing, merchandise handling, and offices. Retail firms must consider sales, warehousing, and office space requirements. Service firms must have appropriate office, conference, filing, and research areas.

Manufacturing Concerns

Manufacturing firms need to understand how sales volume affects the needs for both product production and warehousing of raw materials and finished products. The best way of examining this problem is the process of walking around. This consists of physically walking through the production and warehousing areas at several different times of day, several different days of the week, and several different weeks of the year. One should be looking for choke points and dead areas: places where space is inadequate for the volume of work being done, or space that is standing idle as work proceeds elsewhere. If one finds that there is insufficient space for the process, then one must ask whether more space is needed, or whether rearranging the process will eliminate the choke point. Conversely, if one finds that there is unused space, one must ask what profitable use can be made of this space. Both situations are problems. Insufficient space may well preclude being able to expand the business to take advantage of business opportunities. Too much space means that money is being spent on unproductive assets.

There are remedies for both situations. Too little space may be solved by making the process more efficient, by building additional facilities, or by outsourcing some or all of the production. Too much space may be addressed by dividing the facility and renting the surplus space. One may also move the business to space that is appropriately sized; however, moving a business is always a very expensive undertaking and it disrupts business. Moving should be considered a last resort when other approaches have failed.

Retail Concerns

An old saw about retail business is that there are only three things that determine success: location, location, and location. Certainly, while there is more to success than simply being in the right place at the right time, there is truth to that saying. Location *is* extremely important to retail businesses.

What makes a location good? One very important factor is the amount of traffic—either people walking or automobiles driving—that pass the location during hours of business. Another factor is the visibility of the location to the traffic: Is the storefront and the signage identifying the store situated in such a way that people passing cannot help but see the business?

Statistics concerning traffic are available from a variety of sources. State, county, and local highway authorities usually collect and maintain very accurate counts of the number of automobiles that use a street or road at any given time of day. Property owners, especially the owners and managers of shopping malls, usually collect and maintain statistics concerning the number of automobiles in the parking lot and the number of people in the mall at various times of day. Local business groups and commercial property real estate brokers collect and maintain such statistics as an aid to property value appraisal and for promoting business districts. Governmental agencies are required to disclose this data to citizens; other groups may charge for the information or may restrict its use in various ways.

Of course, simply having a large number of automobiles passing by is not an adequate measure of retail traffic. Access to the store for the traffic, the speed of the traffic, and the nature of the traffic are critical factors. A site along a restricted access highway where thousands of automobiles pass at seventy-five miles per hour on their way to the next city has little value as a retail location. Drivers in such traffic are very unlikely to stop where access is inconvenient. Similarly, a four lane urban thoroughfare that allows no left turns across the oncoming lanes restricts the useful retail traffic to only those automobiles that can turn right off the traffic lanes into the parking area. An ideal location is one near an intersection of local traffic streets, marked with either a stop sign or a traffic light that requires the automobiles to slow in front of the business. If the drivers are slowing for the light, they are likely to decide to stop at the store. On the other side of the light, drivers are likely to continue accelerating away. An ideal location also allows advertising signs that are highly visible from the intersection. Drivers are unlikely to go searching for retail shops; rather, they tend to stop at the closest visible store. A site as little as a city block from a busy intersection may have little value as a retail location unless large, attention-grabbing signs, easily visible from the intersection, are allowed.

Mall locations have a similar, but different set of traffic concerns. One very important question to answer about mall locations is, "Who is in this mall?" A mall frequented primarily by blue-collar shoppers is most likely inappropriate for a gourmet wine and cheese shop. Conversely, a high-income area is not suited for discount outlets: There are no Wal-Marts in New Greenwich, Connecticut! Managers of malls continually collect demographic data about the people who frequent their space. Survey data is taken to determine the ages, income level, gender, employment, spending patterns, frequency of visiting the mall, distance that people travel to get to the mall, and so on. Thus mall locations offer market research resources that are expensive or impossible to obtain for freestanding sites. One may peruse the data collected by the mall managers to determine the fit between the people who frequent the mall and the product or service that the business provides.

It may be somewhat surprising to know that all locations within any single mall are not equally valuable. Every retail mall has regular patterns to the traffic of people within it. Determinates of the traffic patterns include (a) the location of the entries to the mall from parking lots, (b) location of anchor stores (i.e., large department stores in the mall), (c) the location of food courts, movie theaters, and toilets, (d) the location of escalators and stairs, and (e) the grouping of similar stores, such as apparel or furniture stores, within the mall. As with demographic information, mall managers usually have data concerning traffic patterns within the mall.

Regardless, there is no substitute for an on-site inspection of the mall itself. This inspection should include visiting the mall at different times throughout the day to observe variations in traffic. All levels of the mall should be examined. The number of empty store spaces should be counted. If any such spaces have signs proclaiming that a particular business will be "coming soon!" the business owner or franchiser should be contacted. Are they *really* going to open a store there? If so, when? If the prior occupant of any empty space can be found, ask why they vacated the space: Former tenants are often the most reliable source of information concerning mall traffic, maintenance, and management.

One advantage to good mall locations is that a business may well be able to gain synergy from being in close proximity to complementary stores. For example, a mall may well have a bridal shop. Nearby will be a florist, a card shop, and a bakery. The bride-to-be can register at stores within the mall for crystal, china, and linens. The mall photography shop may handle the wedding pictures. Similar synergies often exist for automotive after-market items, for consumer electronics, for home furnishings and decorating, and for many, many other areas.

SIGNAGE AND FRONTAGE CONCERNS

Although many people today are somehow offended by advertising signage, having adequate identifying signs is essential for the success of retail businesses. Quite simply, if a store is difficult to find, few customers will make the effort to shop there, and the business will fail. It seems that citizens want *no* signs, at all, except for that particular business for which the citizen is currently looking.

Despite customers' reliance on location signs, many communities have passed extremely restrictive sign codes. The presence of large, attention-demanding signs is no indication that the business being considered can have similar signage. Often, restrictive sign codes grandfather existing signage, allowing them to remain, while prohibiting any new signs. Such covenants often require that all signage be brought into conformity with the code if any of several events occur: if a specified amount of time, from the adoption of the sign code, has passed; if the business changes ownership or location; if the sign requires significant maintenance; or if some percentage of existing signs are either removed or brought into conformity. The *only* way to determine what will be allowed is to make a trip to the sign inspection department of the city, county, or state government, as appropriate. Signs are regulated as to size, location, content, and construction method by all levels of government. There is even a federal law, the Highway Beautification Act, that regulates billboards along any federally funded highway. The best way to evaluate signage restrictions is to obtain copies of the code from the controlling government, read the code, and discuss its enforcement with the sign inspectors. Local sign manufacturers are familiar with sign codes and restrictions. Sign companies exist to sell signs and managers will be glad to discuss sign needs and restrictions with prospective buyers of a business. If the business being considered for acquisition depends on specific signage, obtain *written* confirmation from the inspection department that the proposed signage conforms to the relevant code, and make the obtaining of necessary permits a condition of purchase.

All shopping malls have some sign requirements as provisions of leasing store space. Often, signs may be obtained solely from a sign supplier approved by the mall management or owners. Such provisions always act to increase the cost of location signage. The only way to determine the effect of mall restrictions is to discuss them fully with the leasing agent, obtaining exact copies of the relevant restrictions as a part of any lease agreement.

Frontage is essential to any retail business not located in a shopping mall. There are two items of concern: access and parking. As discussed, it is not enough to be on a high-traffic highway: The business must be on a high-traffic highway where people can get off. And when they get off, there must be a place to park their cars. Businesses fail because of inadequate parking. In the 1970s and 1980s, many towns, in an effort to preserve the downtown shopping areas, closed the main streets, turning them into pedestrian malls. Parking was located off the main street, any-where from a half-block to several blocks away. All this redevelopment was done with revenue bonds, which means that the development had to generate funds to pay for the construction bonds. Because of this, all the parking was made metered parking. This meant that there was a two- to four-hour limit on parking, and failure to feed the meter resulted in a $5 to $10 fine. The parking usually was not convenient to the downtown stores. Most often, it was not easy to get into the stores. Occasionally, stores made back entrances from the parking areas, but usually shoppers had to walk from the parking lots around the old streets to get to the original entrances.

Most customers simply choose to go to the suburban malls. There, parking was free; there were no parking limits or fines; entrances to the stores were close and convenient. Downtown stores failed. Cities de-faulted on their revenue bonds. Today, few of these downtown malls re-main. In the last few years most have been returned to auto traffic streets. Despite this well-intentioned effort, very few downtown areas have re-gained any retail shopping of significance.

As with many of the investigation issues in mergers and acquisitions, frontage, access, and parking can be best determined by a physical in-spection of the location. There simply is no substitute for a careful and exhaustive visit to the site. The number and size of entrance drives can be measured. One may observe if there are impediments to access, such as prohibited left turns, center medians that cannot be crossed, high-speed traffic that makes getting into and out of the parking area difficult and dangerous, an inadequate number of parking spaces, or parking spaces that are restricted to use by permit holders. Existing signs can be examined and photographed. The location can be approached from vari-ous directions to evaluate, firsthand, the visibility and access of the site. Ideally, several site visits would be made at different times of day, at dif-ferent days of the week, and at various dates during the year. As a practical matter, most acquisitions of businesses occur in fairly short periods, precluding any such exhaustive investigation of the location. It is necessary, therefore, to depend on secondary sources for much of the site evaluation.

Although much information can be obtained from government sources, real estate brokers, and mall management, the information must be evaluated critically. Government data are often dated. There usually is no person held responsible for its accuracy or completeness. Data from real estate agents and mall management are produced to sell lease space. Although it may not be fraudulent, such information is usually slanted to meet the purposes of the leasing agents.

One must be quite skeptical of demographic claims. Not only does mall management have an interest in presenting the most favorable picture of the mall, but there is also no audit of the responses of those surveyed. Often people are less than completely honest answering survey questions. They tend to exaggerate the amount of income they have, to reduce their age by a few years, and generally to slant answers to impress the surveyor. The authors of this book have examined many such studies over the last 30 years. Not once have we seen a mall study that did not claim that 65% of the people visiting the mall were between the ages of 18 and 35, and had an average family income 10% to 20% above the median family income in the United States. In many cases, a visit to the mall in the morning disclosed that the mall was filled with elderly people who were using the public areas for exercise walking. An evening visit found the mall filled with unsupervised groups of teenagers, engaged in loud talk, playing loud music, and horseplay. Certainly, neither of these groups is somehow unworthy, but it is obvious that they do not meet the demographics furnished by the mall management.

Several sources of reliable demographic information are provided at the end of this chapter.

LEASE TERMS

Lease terms are highly variable. Anything that is not specifically illegal may be made part of the contract. Lease payments may include or exclude items such as construction, furnishings, displays, maintenance, snow removal from parking areas, heating and air conditioning, and taxes and insurance.

Some leases simply contract that a specific number of periodic payments of cash will be made. Some leases, especially in retail malls, have, in addition to the minimum periodic payment requirement, provisions for an additional payment, based on a percentage of the business's gross sales, which is to be made either monthly or quarterly. Percentage of sales leases have significant implications for the conduct of a retail business. Such provisions tend to discourage discounting and promotion. Attempts to increase gross sales entail either price reductions as inducements to buy, or cost increases for advertising and promotional items. Gross sales increase, increasing lease payments; however, margins are reduced, restricting the ability to pay the increased lease amount. Such leases also reduce the confidentiality of business information. When a lease requires percentage payments, there is invariably a provision giving the lessor the right periodically to examine the books of the lessee. If the lessor is required to disclose financial statements to stockholders or to limited partners, it is often possible to estimate quite accurately the sales of individual lessors from the information disclosed. Both situations, having to allow examination of books and public disclosure by the lessor, increase the possibility of sensitive business information being made available to competitors.

Lease requirements may also reduce the discretion of the owner to do business. In malls, there are often restrictions on lessees concerning the types of merchandise that may be offered for sale. Often, mall leases require that stores be periodically remodeled. During the remodeling, the store may well have to be closed, effectively putting the store out of business for a period of time. This is quite expensive, not only in cash outlays, but also in lost traffic during and immediately after the remodeling.

Another common lease requirement is that the business owner personally guarantee the lease payments. This means that if the business is unsuccessful and lease payments cannot be made out of business revenues, the lessor will expect payments from the personal assets of the business owner. Most leases for retail space are multi-year. The entire sum of lease payments may be due, without regard to the success of the business. Thus the requirement to personally guarantee a lease greatly reduces its value to the prospective purchaser of a business.

In one common type of lease, called a *net lease,* the landlord pays only the taxes on the property. There are also leases, called *net-net leases,* in which the landlord pays both taxes and utilities. Most often, in both types of leases, the lessee is responsible for ordinary maintenance of items within the leased space, such as carpet cleaning, while the landlord is responsible for maintenance of extraordinary items, such as storm damage, and of common areas, such as window cleaning and sweeping the parking lot.

An examination of the existing lease document will disclose the current lease arrangement. In exercising due diligence, one must question if the lease is appropriately structured and priced. One measure of appropriateness is that the lease is consistent with current market conditions for the area. This can be determined by interviewing commercial real estate brokers who have comparable properties available. Competition forces agents both to know their market and to offer going rates to prospective customers. If the current lease is not consistent with the market, then the business either is overpaying or is getting a bargain. Regardless, the prospective buyer of the business needs to know what the lease conditions are.

The lease must also be examined carefully for assignability. Often, purchasing a business does not entitle the new owners to take over the existing lease. The lessor may have retained rights either to approve the new owner, to increase the lease payments, or to require an entirely new lease agreement. Because leases are enforceable contracts under the Uniform Commercial Code, one should have a lawyer examine the lease prior to accepting any assignment of its terms.

Certainly lease terms are an area for serious negotiation during the acquisition process. Unfavorable leases can be quite costly, and may, in fact, render a proposed acquisition unacceptable. On the other hand, favorable lease terms are often undervalued by the sellers, providing an unexpected bargain for the prospective buyer.

COMPETING AND COMPLEMENTARY BUSINESSES

A final consideration in an investigation of location is the existence of competing and complementary businesses. This is a problematic area. It is well known that there is a synergy to be gained from proximity with complementary businesses. For this reason it is rare to see a single franchise restaurant in an area. Franchise fast food operators deliberately attempt to locate close to each other. First, what makes a good location for one restaurant makes a good location for others. Second, while Wendy's may well be competing for food dollars with Kentucky Fried Chicken, Pizza Hut, and Taco Bell, the fact is that because each store sells a different type of food, across time all the stores will have increased traffic by being close to each other. However, one rarely sees a Wendy's, Hardee's, and McDonald's all together. All of these stores sell primarily the same product: hamburgers. They are direct competitors, offering essentially identical products, and so they do not experience increased sales from proximity with each other, as do complementary businesses.

The same phenomenon leads to the Chevrolet, Ford, and Chrysler dealers all being in the same part of town. It is common for similar businesses to be primarily located in a particular part of town, as with auto dealerships. If you are going to be in a business that is predominately located in a certain area, then there is usually a disadvantage to being outside the area. Customers expect to find that particular type of business in the customary area and will tend to restrict shopping to those firms located there.

When examining a business for acquisition, therefore, the location must also be evaluated for both competing and complementary businesses. If the business is an auto parts store, it will probably not be desirable for the business nextdoor to be a NAPA auto parts store. On the other hand, if several garages are close by, one may experience increased business both by selling to the other garages and from the increased traffic of people doing maintenance on their cars. Competing and complementary businesses are important in mall locations, as well. Although a bridal shop will benefit from having other apparel shops nearby, most likely the owners would prefer to have the sole bridal shop in the mall.

SUGGESTED READINGS

American Production and Inventory Control Society. (1997). *Selected readings in small manufacturing*. Falls Church, VA: APICS, the Educational Society for Resource Management.
Cedarleaf, J. (1994). *Plant layout and flow improvement*. New York: McGraw-Hill.
Harbour, J. L. (1996). *Cycle time reduction: Designing and streamlining work for high performance*. New York: Quality Resources.
Jackson, H. K., Jr., & Frigon, N. L. (1998). *A practical guide to capacity planning and management*. New York: Wiley.
Ramaswamy, R. (1996). *Design and management of service processes*. Reading, MA: Addison-Wesley.

8 | Insurance for the Business

Insurance can be a large problem for small businesses. In many cases, insurance is expensive. However, not having insurance can lead to business failure in the event of catastrophe or litigation. Although there have been recent efforts by Congress to limit the awards that can be made in lawsuits against various businesses, judgments that are astronomical in size continue to be made. Maintaining insurance provides a small business owner with two protections: First, the insurance will pay the cost of catastrophes or litigation judgments to the extent of the policy. Second, in the case of litigation, the insurance company will aggressively act to limit the amount of the judgment against the business, providing expert council in tort litigation. Although there are many, many types of insurance, this discussion will be limited to business's big four: (1) product liability, (2) employee health care, (3) workers' compensation, and (4) property and casualty (McShane, 1996).

PRODUCT LIABILITY INSURANCE

Product liability and professional liability insurance provides coverage for any harm—physical, mental, or financial—caused by the product or service of a firm. If anyone is hurt, injured, or killed by the product, or if any of these events occur near where the product is being used, the company that manufactured the product most likely will be sued. In fact, the safe bet is that the company *will* be sued. Whether or not the suit results in a judgment against the business, lawsuits are expensive and take management time and effort that could be better expended on business issues.

Product liability judgments are often so large that they exceed the total value of the firm. Huge judgments have driven the cost of product liability insurance to very high levels. In the 1970s, product liability insurance for small single-engine airplanes become so great that it exceeded the actual construction cost for the planes ("General Aviation," 1988). The cost of product liability insurance was cited as a major factor in Cessna's, Piper's, and Beechcraft's decisions to cease production of single-engine planes. These companies only recently resumed production of such aircraft (Banks, 1994), subsequent to legislation that greatly limits the manufacturer's product liability. It is unfortunate that such limits do not exist for other businesses. Thus the specter remains of million-dollar judgments for events managers cannot hope to control, such as customers who pour hot coffee into their own laps! The crux of product liability is that businesses can be held liable for the stupidity of all who might use or be near the product. A prudent business manager will seek to limit the business's potential loss from litigation. Product liability insurance provides one means to limit such losses.

When investigating a business as a potential merger or acquisition, the first question concerning product or professional liability insurance is whether or not product liability insurance is available for this industry, business, or product. There are several businesses and products for which product liability is either prohibitively expensive or not available at any cost. Examples of uninsurable businesses include tree trimming and thrill rides, such as carnival rides, parachute jumping, and personal watercraft rental. An example of an uninsurable product is a diving board for a backyard swimming pool.

If product or professional liability insurance is available, it must be examined for premiums, terms, coverage, and the strength and stability of the insuring organization. Some risky and thus hard-to-insure businesses carry insurance through mutual policies sponsored by trade organizations. Such insurance may be of limited value in the event of a serious damage suit. Often the insurance is very restricted in coverage, and the insuring organization lacks sufficient financial resources to cover lengthy litigation or large awards. Any costs not covered must come from the capital of the business.

If the business does not have a product or professional liability insurance policy, one must determine why there is no policy. Is insurance unavailable? If so, why? Or perhaps the business has never been sued, and thus management has not recognized the need for liability insurance. The fact that a given business has avoided suit is no indication of the riskiness —or safety—of a given activity. Airline flight attendants have been pouring hot coffee onto passengers for years without any sizable damage awards being made. Still, McDonald's was hit with a million-dollar judgment when a customer was scalded by a cup of hot coffee she tucked between her legs before driving over a speed bump.

The issue of product and professional liability is extremely serious for small businesses, which lack the financial resources either to fight unjust suits or to absorb large awards. McDonald's scarcely noticed the effect of paying a million-dollar award, and in fact may have benefited from the tremendous amount of publicity the award engendered. A single-site restaurant would most likely have been driven to bankruptcy by such an award, absent product liability insurance.

EMPLOYEE HEALTH CARE

Employee health care is a rapidly increasing cost for those businesses that provide it to their employees. As recently as 15 years ago, only the largest firms in the Unites States offered health care as an employee benefit. Today, it is commonly provided by even the smallest businesses as a benefit necessary to attract and keep qualified employees. Over the last 10 years, the cost of health care has increased at a rate more than double that of overall inflation. Despite the current interest and effort being expended to reduce the rate of health care cost increases, successfully containing health care costs is problematic. It seems likely that both the pressures to provide health care for employees and the cost of doing so will continue to mount. Thus this issue must be carefully examined when evaluating a merger or acquisition candidate.

There are several ways in which health coverage may be provided. Large companies typically are self-insured. Such firms usually contract with a large insurer, such as Aetna or Connecticut General, to administer health coverage, but pay all costs directly. Smaller firms generally negotiate with insurance companies to obtain coverage at a fixed premium. The smallest firms often find that affordable coverage can be obtained only through trade organizations, which negotiate with insurance coverage to obtain favorable rates by pooling employees of associated businesses.

Regardless of the form of coverage, one must be aware that current law makes it extremely difficult to reduce or eliminate health coverage once it has been provided. In fact, the Supreme Court, in a 7 to 2 decision, recently ruled that it is illegal to dismiss employees in order to eliminate or reduce employee benefits (Felsenthal, 1997). Thus if health coverage is offered, a safe assumption is that it will continue to be a cost of doing business. If it is not offered, it may well become necessary in the near future.

WORKERS' COMPENSATION

Workers' compensation is a mandatory coverage, required in all 50 states. It provides income for workers who are injured on the job. In form, workers' compensation is both a quasi-tax and quasi-self-insurance: It is neither a tax nor self-insurance, but has elements of both. Premiums for workers' compensation are collected by the state. The amount of the premium is a percentage of payroll costs, determined by the historical rates of compensation paid within the state by the industry and by the particular business in the industry. Thus businesses where injury is more likely, such as sign erection, pay higher rates for workers' compensation than do businesses where on-the-job injuries are uncommon. However, the rate will vary among sign erectors, depending upon the individual business's historical rate and the severity of injury.

There are several sources of information concerning workers' compensation for any individual business. First, one may simply examine the payments made for previous years. Second, workers' compensation claims are public record: One may examine such claims at the appropriate agency office. Third, workers' compensation claims are related to the safety of the workplace. The record of OSHA inspections and citations may well identify problem areas and provide a basis to evaluate likely future claims.

PROPERTY AND CASUALTY INSURANCE

Compared to the three types of insurance discussed above, property and casualty insurance is minor. Such coverage is usually relatively inexpensive and is almost always carried by the business, if only because the mortgage holder on the buildings requires that such coverage be maintained. Nevertheless, the existence of property and casualty insurance should be confirmed, and the amounts, limits, copayments, and premiums determined.

For some businesses, property and casualty insurance can be a significant cost. Businesses located in earthquake- and flood-prone areas often find that insurance is expensive and hard to obtain. Of course, the more likely it is that a casualty will occur, the more insurance is needed. Certainly, if the business being considered is located in California, the risk of earthquake must be considered. However, the strongest earthquake ever recorded in the United States took place in southeastern Missouri, not in California! Floods occur in unlikely places as well. If a business is located in a flood plain, behind levees, floods will obviously be a consideration. But floods can occur on high ground, far from any creek or river. In 1996, businesses in both Chicago and New York City were flooded when water mains broke.

Insurance is a major operating cost for most businesses. Although only the four most common types of insurance coverage are discussed here, there are other forms that might be relevant to the operation of any particular business. All existing insurance policies must be examined to determine premium cost, coverage, and limitations. The operating risks of a business must be evaluated in order to determine that the appropriate forms and amounts of insurance are being carried.

One way to approach the task of analyzing the insurance needs and coverage of a business being considered is to retain a risk manager as a consultant. The issue of business insurance is so complex that even CPAs are counseled to seek expert assistance before making recommendations to a client (Fleming, 1996).

SUGGESTED READINGS

Bury, D., & Heischman, L. (1994). *The buyer's guide to business insurance* (edited by Camille Akin). Grant's Pass, OR: Oasis Press/PSI Research.

Goodden, R. L. (1996). *Preventing and handling product liability.* New York: Dekker.

Malecki, D. S., et al. (1995). *Commercial liability insurance and risk management* (3d ed.). Malvern, PA: American Institute for Chartered Property Casualty Underwriters.

Williams, C. A., Jr., Smith, M. L., & Young, P. C. (1998). *Risk management and insurance.* Boston: Irwin/McGraw-Hill.

9 | Valuation of Short-Term Assets

When Hendrix Niemann bought Automatic Door Specialists, he discovered that "there were a lot of bad receivables on the books. Close to *half* were more than 90 days old, and the majority of that dated from 1988," nearly two years earlier (Niemann, 1990, p. 36).

Niemann met with the seller, Peter Klosky; Automatic Door Specialists' senior employee, Darvin Brothers, who was helping him in the negotiations; and his own accountant to assign value the company's inventory. "Peter Klosky couldn't do anything at this point about overripe receivables," wrote Niemann, "but he was bound and determined to get every last cent out of this junk heap he called his shop."

"There's usable stuff in there, Darvin," Peter said.

"Peter, that's just old pieces of lumber. We're not going to pay you for that!" Darvin replied.

Peter pulled open a drawer crammed with wires, gears, and old circuit boards. "There's value in here, Darvin," he said.

"There's nothing in there, Peter."

"Give me $25 for this drawer," Peter said.

"$5."

"$10," Peter countered.

"$8."

"OK," Peter said. "But I still say there's value in there" (pp. 36-37).

When a business is purchased, regardless of whether it is structured as a purchase of stock or as a bulk purchase, what is acquired is often described as a bundle of assets and liabilities. The value of what is actually purchased is the residual of the things of positive value to the purchaser—that is, the ~~assets~~—minus the things of negative value, the *liabilities*.

Accountants define assets as probable future economic benefits obtained or controlled by a particular entity as a result of past transactions or events (FASB, 1996, paragraph 25). Liabilities are defined as probable future sacrifices of economic benefits arising from present obligations of a particular entity to transfer assets or provide services to other entities in the future as a result of past transactions or events (FASB, 1996, paragraph 35). In other words, assets and liabilities are things, either material or intangible, expected to be of economic value in the future.

The problem in examining a business for the purpose of merger or acquisition is to determine the amount of *current* economic value to assign to both assets and liabilities, which by definition are things expected to have *future* value. This process of valuation is, obviously, the heart of the acquisition process. The buyer would like to assign the lowest possible value, thus reducing the price of the business. The seller, on the other hand, would prefer the highest possible value in order to receive a higher price. Only when the buyer and seller agree upon the valuation can a transaction take place.

Assets and liabilities are commonly categorized as being either short-term or long-term. A short-term asset or liability is one that has an economic value expected to be realized within one year or one operating cycle of the business, whichever is greater. A long-term asset or liability is one that has an economic value *not* expected to be realized for more than one year or one operating cycle. Additionally, an asset can be either physical, such as inventory, machinery, or buildings, or an asset can be intangible, such as rights to a license, trademark, or patent. Liabilities may be a specific dollar amount that is owed by the business, regardless of future events, or a liability may be contingent upon some future event, such as the conclusion of a lawsuit. We shall discuss each type of asset and liability, and the problems of assessing the appropriate value of each.

CASH

The term *cash*, as used in business, means more than simply currency or dollar bills. In fact, most businesses keep only small amounts of currency on premises, unless there is a specific, immediate need to do so.

The *cash* of a business is composed of the currency and coin held, bank deposits, checks, drafts, and money orders: that is, anything that a bank would be expected to accept at face value for deposit.

Cash is valued at its face value: A dollar bill is worth one dollar, a hundred-dollar bill is worth one hundred dollars. In fact, cash is the medium by which all assets and liabilities are measured. The process of valuation is simply one of assigning a particular dollar amount to each asset and liability. If the valuation is being done in a country other than the United States, valuation is a process of assigning money amounts to assets and liabilities, in the money unit of that country.

All businesses need some amount of cash. Cash must be available to make change for customers, to pay suppliers and employees, to pay taxes, and to pay dividends to owners. The amount of cash needed varies from business to business, depending upon the nature and size of the business.

Thus cash is the simplest asset to value and the easiest to confirm. Cash physically present within the business can be counted at the time of change of ownership. Cash on deposit with financial institutions will be counted and confirmed by the holding institution. Cash is also the asset least likely to be damaged or spoiled. As it exists primarily in bookkeeping records of the business and of the depository institution, cash is not often subject to rot, mildew, or catastrophe, short of an economic failure of the country issuing the money. This is not true of other assets.

INVENTORY

Inventory consists of goods held within the business either for use in the process of the business or for direct sale to customers. The question to be answered in examining the business for acquisition is how much money can be obtained by selling, in an orderly manner, the inventory currently owned by the business. This is usually not an easy question to answer. For some inventory, such as grain held by an elevator operator or farmer, the process is simple and obvious: The seller has no negotiation power because grain sells at prices set in open auction markets, reported instantly by services that record and handle every transaction within an exchange. For most businesses, however, inventory is not a commodity indistinguishable from that of every other supplier. The price at which the inventory will sell is subject to a wide range of uncertain variables, including fashion changes, competition, condition of the inventory, ability of the sales force, the success of efforts to differentiate the product from those of competitors, and economic conditions.

Although the books of the firm being examined will include a valuation for the inventory on hand, the book value cannot be accepted as either accurate or authoritative. There are several methods available to management for assigning a value to inventory for purposes of financial reporting. The most common methods used to value inventory include (a) specific identity, (b) FIFO (First-In-First-Out), (c) LIFO (Last-In-First-Out), (d) lower of cost or market, and (e) weighted average. All five of these inventory valuing methods are acceptable for purposes of both income tax and external reporting, yet each method arrives at a different value for inventory. None may be the economic value that a purchaser of the business would be willing to pay. Additionally, there are several inventory valuing methods that are *not* acceptable for income tax or external reporting, but which are used by management for internal control purposes, including NIFO (Next-In-First-Out), base stock, standard cost, and variable cost.

Thus a prospective purchaser of a business must understand the implications of the inventory valuation system being used by the business being considered. A thorough discussion, however, of the various methods of inventory valuation is beyond the scope of this book. If more information is desired, any intermediate cost or managerial accounting text will include both a description of each method and references to guide further study.

For the purposes of the exercise of due diligence, it is imperative that one be physically present during a periodic inventory of the business being considered. A complete walk-through should be made of all areas where inventory is stored. This physical examination includes looking for signs of old or misvalued inventory, such as dusty, dirty, or torn packages. The accumulation of dust and dirt might indicate that the inventory is not selling, even though it is being carried on the books at full value. Torn, scuffed, and worn packaging might indicate a product that has been returned, either because it did not sell or because it failed in use and was returned for warranty. Careful note should be made of model numbers and of product features of inventory items. In fashion and technology businesses, last period's "hot" merchandise may well be this period's scrap. Many resellers of small computers have failed because technological change rendered inventory obsolete before it could be sold.

Obsolescence is another difficult issue that must be considered in determining the value of inventory. Obsolescence occurs because of fashion, technological, or business changes. Sometimes the difference between a fashion and a technological change is ambiguous. One would be hard-pressed to identify specific technological advances in a particular model of automobile between any two consecutive years; however, once this year's model is offered for sale, last year's model is suddenly worth much less, although it is still a new automobile. Occasionally, inventory is obsolete only in that management has made a decision to abandon a specific line of business. Thus a retailer who has abandoned the large appliance market may have refrigerators and ranges in inventory that are obsolete only insofar as they no longer fit the business strategy. Regardless of their fashion or technological currency, the appliances most likely will not be sold for the amount at which they are valued on the books of the business.

Once the inventory of the business has been accurately identified and counted, a value must be placed on it. This value has little or no relationship to the value that may be assigned for income tax or financial reporting purposes. As a purchaser of a business, one should *not* be willing to pay any more for inventory than its actual market value, adjusted for selling and handling costs. What the business originally paid for the inventory is irrelevant to its current value. The book value of the inventory is based upon accounting rules that generally work to assign the lowest reasonable value to inventory, based upon its original purchase cost as determined by original sales documents. The current economic value of inventory may well be either greater or less than the accounting book value. The value to be assigned *must* be that value the inventory currently has for the business being acquired.

ACCOUNTS RECEIVABLE

For most firms, accounts receivable are the largest intangible asset of the business. Accounts receivable are debts that are owed to the business by customers for services rendered or products sold. The issue for a purchaser of a business is to gauge how much of the amount shown in such accounts will actually be collectable. A sad fact of business is that all debts are not collected. People fail to pay for a variety of reasons, including inability to pay, disputes over the service or product furnished, disputes over the amount owed, and failure of the business to attempt to collect. Thus the gross amount of accounts receivable shown in the books may well be either more than can actually be collected, which is the common circumstance, or less, which is a more rare condition.

The technique most used to estimate the amount of uncollectable accounts receivable is to examine the collection history of the firm. Such an examination can take several forms. One way is to compare each year's credit sales to that year's collection on accounts receivable. The method most used by managerial accountants is called *account aging*. This is a process of collecting a historical record of accounts that become past due and calculating subsequent collections made on those past-due accounts. In this way, highly accurate estimates of the amount that will be uncollectable can be made based upon just how delinquent the account has become. If normal account terms are net amount due in 30 days, and an account is 180 days past due, it is highly unlikely that the account will ever be collected.

The examination of accounts receivable should focus on old past-due accounts. One should carefully examine the record of collection efforts. It is not at all uncommon to find that, other than sending a monthly statement, no effort has been made to collect the amount due. Sometimes a phone call or a letter from the firm's attorney will result in complete payment. Accounts that are past due might also be turned over to a collection agency. A sample of past-due accounts and of accounts that have been written off should be traced to the debtors. Questions that should be answered concerning past due business accounts include the following: (a) Is the debtor business still operating? (b) Was a judgment obtained against the debtor business? (c) Is there collateral property that may be seized to satisfy the debt? (d) Is the business still a customer, despite having not paid in the past? (e) Is there an unresolved dispute concerning the service, product, or amount owed?

Another consideration concerning accounts receivable when a business changes its ownership is that some debtors will see the change of ownership as an opportunity not to pay the owed amounts. Some will attempt to exploit the situation by offering to pay only part of what is due, if they are to remain customers of the new owners. Unfortunately, those unlikely to pay can rarely be identified in advance. Some may be customers who were loyal to the old managers, but now feel free to change suppliers, refusing to pay the owed amounts. Others may suddenly "discover" that there are disputes concerning services, products, or charges, secure in the belief that the outgoing management is unlikely to be loyal to the new owners and will not challenge the false allegations. Some may just believe that the unpaid bills may be overlooked in the office turmoil that invariably accompanies a change in ownership.

The failure to collect accounts receivable can be critical to the success of the purchase or acquisition. Most businesses—and all small businesses—operate within a critical cash flow situation. If the success of a business plan and projected cash flows is dependent upon collecting existing accounts receivable, not collecting them can lead to business failure and bankruptcy.

One potential way to investigate these account receivable issues is to call upon an expert: a factor. Factors are businesses that exist solely to make discount purchases of accounts receivable from businesses. The factor then collects the accounts, making a profit on the difference between the amount paid and the amount collected. The business receives immediate cash for the accounts receivable, and is relieved of the costs and risk of collection. Another way to avoid problems is simply not to purchase the accounts receivable as part of the business. The price of the business is reduced by some amount equivalent to the value of the receivables; the sellers then keep the rights to the accounts receivable, and may either collect them or sell them to a factor. Neither of these options allows a prospective buyer to avoid the investigation of accounts receivable, but both may work to ease negotiations and to reduce subsequent costs and risks of collection.

Other short-term assets that may be part of the business include such things as prepaid costs—that is unexpired insurance, property taxes, and leases. Sometimes there are investments in stocks, bonds, or other securities that can readily be sold for cash. All of these assets must be examined in a similar manner to accounts receivable to ascertain their current value to the business.

Thus the exercise of due diligence in examining short-term assets includes the four-step process of (1) identifying specific assets, (2) investigating the assets for existence, condition, and ownership rights, (3) determining the current value of the assets to the business, and (4) deciding whether ownership of the assets is to be transferred with the business.

SUGGESTED READINGS

Damodaran, A. (1996). *Investment valuation: Tools and techniques for determining the value of any asset.* New York: Wiley.

Public Sector Committee, International Federation of Accountants. (1995). *Definition and recognition of assets.* New York: International Federation of Accountants.

10 | Valuation of Long-Term Assets

"**I** was about to sign a long-term lease on the building," Hendrix Niemann wrote, "because I was getting a five-year, no-rent-increase deal."

"Don't!" he was warned. "It's a firetrap. The boiler is ancient and ready to blow . . . the building has no hot water. There is a rat's nest (literally) in the owner's closet" (Niemann, 1990, p. 36).

Certainly, most business acquisitions transpire with fewer unpleasant surprises than did the purchase of Automatic Door Specialists. All business acquisitions are fraught with problems, however. One intractable problem complicates every business acquisition: deciding just how much the things that constitute the business are actually worth. This problem is particularly difficult for long-term assets because there is no ready market in which values are determined.

So what value should Niemann have assigned to the lease of the rat-infested building? Consider the following: A five-year lease with a guarantee of level rent payments provides a certainty concerning future cash requirements that is most unusual for small businesses to have. But, would Niemann be responsible for repairs, maintenance, and safety (and pest control) of the "firetrap" with a faulty boiler? Would the value of guaranteed rent be offset by exorbitant—and increasing—insurance costs? Given the fragile condition of the premises, what was the probability that the building would even last another five years?

Long-term assets are things that are expected to have future economic benefit to the business over a period of time greater than one year. As with short-term assets, long-term assets may be either physical, such as buildings and machinery, or intangible, such as multiple-year leases and patent rights. Valuing long-term assets is complicated by the fact that the future is unknowable. Reasonable estimates of future economic and social states must be made in order to estimate the current value of assets. Usually the only practical method is to make best-case and worst-case projections, based on historical and current conditions and trends. The value that the entrepreneur is willing to pay lies somewhere between these two extremes.

LONG-TERM LEASES

Long-term leases may or may not be included in the asset section of the balance sheet of the business under consideration. Leases, depending on the rights conveyed, are categorized as either *capital leases* or *operating leases*. Capital leases are distinguished from operating leases by transferring a material ownership interest from the lessor to the lessee. An example of a capital lease is one that provides that title to the asset will be transferred to the lessee at the end of the lease term. Generally, operating leases cause little difficulty in establishing their value for the lessee: The lessee incurs only a single risk, that of making the rental payments; the lessor is responsible for ownership costs, such as maintenance, insurance, and property taxes, and retains the risk that the property might lose value. In contrast, capital leases cause great difficulty in establishing their value. The lessee assumes all or most of the ownership costs and risks in addition to the responsibility of making rental payments. In addition to the problems listed above, a business may have a long-term lease asset, either as lessor or as lessee. The value assigned to a lease depends, in part, on whether the business is lessor or lessee.

Even though operating leases are not part of the asset section of the balance sheet, such leases may have a specific value to both the lessee and lessor. From the point of view of the lessee, a lease may be under market, in that the contractual lease payments are less than what payments for a current lease of an equivalent asset would be. Of course, a lease may well be over market if economic conditions are such that a new lease would provide an equivalent asset at lower lease payments. In either case, the prospective purchaser must identify the specific effect of the lease, compare its terms to current market and adjust the value of the business appropriately.

One must also inspect the property and the lease for the existence and terms of leasehold improvements. Leasehold improvements are changes or additions made by the lessee to the asset, ownership of which reverts to the lessor at the end of the lease term. Leasehold improvements may have a large value to lessees, but it must be recognized that the improvements have a short term of value. Similarly, leasehold improvements may be very valuable to lessors, but will not be shown as an asset on the balance sheet until the lease expires.

EQUIPMENT

The valuation of equipment is a highly complex problem. Value depends on the nature, condition, and location of the equipment. It is common in manufacturing businesses to have self-made equipment for which no ready market exists. If the business were forced to sell the equipment, it would bring only scrap price. In some industries, two very distinct markets exist, one for new equipment, and another for used. In the restaurant business, for example, many new restaurants start business every day; many fail in any period. As a result, there is a constant supply and ready market for used restaurant equipment, which usually sells at a substantial discount from new equipment. To ascertain the current market value of common restaurant equipment, one need only contact a restaurant equipment dealer for quotes. On the other hand, there are only a few businesses that make plastic faces for illuminated advertising signs. New plastic forming businesses are rarely created, and it is rare for one in business to go bankrupt. At any specific point in time it is unlikely that new entrants and failing companies exist simultaneously in this business. The equipment to mold plastic sign faces is custom made, and there is no ready market for used equipment. Establishing the value of the equipment requires expertise and informed judgment. An entrepreneur unfamiliar with the process of vacuum forming plastic sign faces would have to hire the services of a consultant: someone who is experienced in the business.

Unlike accountants and lawyers, consultants to the sign industry cannot be found in every city of the United States. Finding one is a problem in itself. A place to start the search for such a consultant would be in the advertising sections of *Signs of the Times,* an industry journal published by ST Publications, of Cincinnati, Ohio. Another possible source of referrals would be the sales offices of Rholm & Hass, the manufacturers of Plexiglas brand sheet plastics, which are commonly used to make sign faces. A similar process would have to be followed for a business in an industry that includes relatively few participants, such as makers of glass tubing, brewers, or hydroponic farming. The search for informed people would start with industry journals and with suppliers to the industry, and would proceed largely by personal contact and recommendation.

Whether or not there is a market for used equipment, the value of the equipment listed on the balance sheet is of little use in establishing economic value. When equipment is acquired, it normally is entered onto the balance sheet at the acquisition cost. There are, however, conditions that can greatly affect the recorded book value of certain long-term assets, as when (a) assets are acquired by donation, (b) a high, unexpected discovery value of assets already owned is found, (c) permanent impairment of use value to assets already owned is discovered, and (d) revaluations are made during quasi-reorganizations. Properties are often donated to businesses by municipalities or other nonprofit organizations to induce the business to locate in a specific community. Donated property is recorded in the books of the business at its *estimated* market value (APB 29). Property already owned by the business may greatly increase in value because of the discovery of mineral or other natural resources. Depending on circumstances, such property may be written up, increasing the book value (SEC, 1978). When property, including plants and equipment, becomes worth significantly less because of such events as decrease in demand for the products made, obsolescence, or a loss of transportation facilities (e.g., when a rail line to the town is abandoned), it is required to be *written down*: that is, the recorded book value is to reduced. Corporations that have suffered great losses over extended periods of time are permitted to obtain a *fresh start* set of accounting records by adjusting the values of certain asset accounts, which can cause the value of these accounts to vary greatly from their original costs (ARB 43; § 25).

Regardless of the original cost recorded or of adjustments made, recorded book value equals the economic value of an asset only by coincidence. Once the cost is entered into the balance sheet, it is then systematically decreased by depreciation. Other than the four exceptions discussed above, no adjustment is made for actual changes in the market value of an asset. Thus book value agrees with fair market value only by sheerest chance. During the process of due diligence, book value is used only as a reference number in establishing the value of the assets of a business and as an aid in identifying all the assets of the business.

When assigning value to equipment, one must consider installation costs. A piece of equipment may not be particularly expensive; however, it may require extensive preparation, foundation, cooling, electricity supply, fire suppression, or monitoring equipment, which may well be very expensive. Thus the value of the equipment must reflect the cost of the ancillary items required for installation and operation. An example is deep fryers for restaurant use. The fryer itself is not particularly expensive. Most communities, however, require that all deep fryers be installed under a powered vent hood, which includes filters to capture evaporated cooking oils and fire suppression equipment to prevent flash fires. The cost of a stainless steel vent hood with fan, filter, and fire suppression can easily be multiples of the cost of a fryer. Thus the hood itself is a valuable equipment asset to the business. Furthermore, installation of fryers and hoods is expensive, so much so that equipment in the hands of a dealer is worth less than half the value of the equipment installed and ready for use in the business.

In investigating the business, one must also look for surplus equipment. In small and in closely held businesses it is common for equipment to continue to be held, even though it is not in current use. In most cases, such excess equipment is not an asset for new owners; rather, it is a liability. Such equipment represents avoidable costs. If the equipment is not being used, then the cost of maintenance, space occupied, and taxes are drains on the profitability of the business. However, there may be no market for the equipment. It may even be costly to dispose of. However, any excess equipment will be shown on the balance sheet at some value: the residual between original acquisition costs and accumulated depreciation. It is necessary, therefore, to ascertain if such surplus has any economic value that can be realized through a sale, even if for scrap. If not, then the costs of disposal must be estimated. The reported book value then must be adjusted down by both the spurious reported value and the estimated cost of disposal.

There are dealers for most industrial equipment who are reliable sources of information concerning the market value of equipment. For highly customized equipment, for which there is no dealer, one may be able to obtain estimates of construction costs from the original manufacturer or from mechanical or industrial engineers. For self-made equipment, one may make a list of components to be individually priced. In the final analysis, one should know the scrap value of the equipment, disposal costs, and replacement costs. From these elements, a reasonable estimate of value may be made.

In the event that there are assets carried on the books that must be scrapped, the costs can be significant. There are companies that specialize in disposal of equipment and of hazardous materials. A perusal of the local *Yellow Pages* or of industry guides, such as *Thomas Register* or *Hoover's Guide to Private Companies,* will disclose the names of companies that handle disposal problems. A general guide to researching industry information is Hawbaker and Nixon's *Industry and Company Information: Illustrated Search Strategy and Sources* (1991).

LAND AND BUILDINGS

For a business that owns its own locations, the land and buildings may well be the single greatest asset held. However, land and buildings are unique, in that every location differs from all other locations. Further complicating the valuation problem are possible restrictions on the use of the land and property. Such limits are imposed by development restriction covenants, by zoning regulations of state and local governments, and by environmental restrictions of the federal government. Often, a business will have grandfather rights, which allow use and activities that violate regulations passed subsequent to the establishment of the business. If such grandfather rights exist, one must carefully consider whether the rights will be extended to new owners: Grandfathered rights often expire upon any change of ownership. One must also carefully inspect the property for hidden problems. Are there structural defects? Is the roof old and deteriorating? Is there a problem with hazardous materials? At least one business was driven to bankruptcy when it was discovered to be sitting on land contaminated with dioxin. The business had been purchased as a sale of stock, and so there was no former corporate owner to look to for damages.

Location of land is the single greatest determinant of its value. One is reminded of the old joke about the Texas land barons who were bragging about their holdings:

"I've got 30,000 acres of prime ranch land," one stated.

"Why, that's a farm, not a ranch. I've got all Pecos County and half of Sabine," the second retorted.

"Shoot, I got all you guys beat. I hold three acres, free and clear," the third said.

"Three acres!" The others laughed. "That's nothing!"

"Oh, yeah? In downtown Dallas."

Indeed, two otherwise identical parcels of land can have widely—and wildly—different market values, differing solely because one is located in the city center on a major highway interchange and the other miles from town on a dirt road.

There are several approaches to estimating the value of real estate, including looking at (a) comparable sales, (b) discounted future earnings, and (c) replacement costs. Comparable sales simply means finding recent sales of similar properties to use as a basis for estimating the market value of the property being appraised. Discounted future earnings is the process of estimating all future cash flows generated by the property, and applying a discount factor to arrive at a net present value. Replacement costs are estimates of what the cost of purchasing similar land and buildings would be. Each of the appraisal methods employs numerous estimates. Expertise and informed judgment are indispensable in this process.

The investigation process is made easier in that, unlike other assets, it is quite easy to obtain objective, independent appraisals of land and building values. Throughout the United States, and in most of the economically developed areas of the world, there are real estate appraisers who do nothing except study and assign values to land and buildings. There are also firms that specialize in surveying, disclosing, and evaluating environmental and hazardous material concerns. Considering the importance of accurately valuing major assets, it is strongly recommended that the services of expert appraisers be retained to assess the values of the land, buildings, and any environmental problems of the business being considered for acquisition.

SUGGESTED READINGS

Eck, J. R., Baker, W. G., & Ensign, D. (1991). *Asset valuation.* Colorado Springs, CO: Shepard's.

Florio, N. M., & Berkey, L. (1995). *Business asset valuation: Allocation and recovery of investment in business acquisitions.* Boston: Little, Brown.

Fried, D., Schiff, M., & Sondhi, A. C. (1989). *Impairments and write-offs of long-lived assets.* Montvale, NJ: National Association of Accountants.

Peterson, R. H. (1994). *Accounting for fixed assets.* New York: Wiley.

Wolf, F. K., & Fitch, W. C. (1994). *Depreciation systems.* Ames, IA: Iowa State University Press.

11 | Intangible Assets

In 1996, a Florida businessman, Charles (Chuck) Cobb, paid $1.2 million for three assets of the failed airline Pan American World Airways. Cobb, with his partner Martin Shugrue, who had been the trustee for Eastern Airlines in its bankruptcy, planned to establish a new airline flying limited routes from Miami, Florida. They believed that there was an advantage to starting the new airline with assets from the defunct Pan Am.

Certainly, from an entrepreneurial point of view, it seems reasonable to purchase a business rather than to start from zero. At the minimum, purchasing a business means that there is immediate cash flow into the business—or does it?

What were the assets of Pan American World Airways in 1996? It's a pretty short list: airplanes, 0; ticket counters, 0; gates, 0; routes, 0; pilots, 0; flight attendants, 0; mechanics, 0. So what did Cobb and Shugrue get for their $1.2 million? They obtained the rights to the names *Pan American World Airways* and *Pan Am*, and they obtained the rights to the Pan Am "meatball": the blue globe logo that graced every Pan Am airplane from the airline's beginning in 1927 to its demise in 1991. So, for $1.2 million, Cobb and Shugrue could call their new airline Pan Am. They could paint the name and logo on their planes, print them on their stationery, and use them in advertising. They could change the colors, shape, and proportions of the name and logo. And, of course, they could prevent any other company or person from using *Pan American World Airways*, *Pan Am*, or the famed blue meatball.

108

Why in the world would anyone, especially successful businessmen like Cobb and Shugrue, pay so much for so little? Why would they, or anyone, want to call a new airline the same name as a failed airline that had not even flown for five years? Consider the following: Did you recognize the name *Pan Am* when it was printed above? Most likely you did. Pan Am, with TWA and British Airways, was one of the most recognized airline names in the world. What Cobb and Shugrue were buying was immediate brand recognition, impossible to have with a newly minted name. As the airlines Kiwi, Western Pacific, and Vanguard have all discovered, it costs millions of dollars and takes many years to build name recognition among the flying public. An instantly recognized name, even the name of a business failure, is a valuable market asset.

The *Pan Am* name and the blue globe logo are examples of intangible assets: items that have no physical existence, but which are expected to provide economic value in the future. Other examples of intangible assets include investments in stocks and bonds, patent and trademark rights, franchises, and goodwill. Intangible assets such as investments in stocks and patents, which have identities separate from the business and thus can be bought and sold, are called *identifiable*. Intangible assets that have no existence separate from the business, such as goodwill, going concern value, and customer loyalty, are called *unidentifiable*. Intangible assets may either be purchased or internally developed. Quite often, intangible assets are the most valuable assets listed on the balance sheet of a business. However, their existence, rights, and value can be quite difficult to establish with certainty. Thus, even though the discussions of short- and long-term assets have included some issues of specific intangible assets, a general discussion of common intangibles that are problematic for investigating a business is appropriate here.

Intangible assets present two questions that must be answered during the investigation of a business for merger or acquisition. First, what intangible assets exist? Second, what value do these intangible assets have? The problems of answering these two questions are exacerbated by the fact that the most valuable intangible assets, such as patents, name brands, and name recognition, usually are generated internally. Because of this, no value for the intangibles is carried on the balance sheet of the books. Often the intangible is unidentifiable, and cannot be valued separately from the business itself. Unless an exhaustive examination is made of the business for the existence and value of intangibles, the value may end up being misidentified and included in the category of goodwill. Misvaluing intangible assets has led to great failures for both sellers and buyers.

Examples of intangibles that were undervalued, and thus bought at a bargain price, are difficult to find. On the other hand, examples abound of buyers who overvalued intangibles, and as a result paid too much to acquire a firm. Why this is so is no mystery: When the intangibles are undervalued and the firm sold at too low a price, the successor firm starts at an advantage and is usually successful. The buyers prefer to credit the subsequent success to superior management, not to fortuitous purchasing. The sellers, who were willing participants to the transaction, are hard pressed to gain any redress for the undervaluation and, most understandably, are loath to admit under any circumstances that they sold too low. The situation is very different when intangibles are overvalued. When too much is paid for an acquisition, subsequent results are at best disappointing, and at worst disastrous. Debt holders seize assets, the firm enters bankruptcy, and aggrieved stockholders sue everyone involved. Although neither buyers nor sellers are eager to admit to mispricing the acquisition, the public nature of bankruptcy and litigation ensure that the business failure will be known. Stories of litigation, accusations, and justifications are the stuff the 6:00 news is made of!

A recent example of this is the controversy over the formation of Cendant Corp., by the merger of HFS, Inc., and CUC International, which turned into a financial disaster. In early 1998, extensive accounting fraud was discovered in the books of CUC International. Following the disclosure of the fraud, Cendant's shares dropped from $41 to less than $10, resulting in a $29 *billion* loss for investors. A discussion of the resulting lawsuits can be found in the July 28, 1999, issue of the *Wall Street Journal.*

GOODWILL

One of the most difficult intangible assets to value is goodwill. As used by accountants, goodwill has no specific, identifiable business value. Rather, it is assumed to represent some expected above-normal financial return in the future. The amount initially placed on the balance for goodwill is simply the difference between the purchase price for the business and the net estimated fair market value of the identifiable business assets at acquisition. For this reason, goodwill is often referred to as an accounting residual. In fact, goodwill is specifically recognized and included as an asset on the balance sheet only when a business is purchased.

Because goodwill and going concern value have no identifiable existence separate from the business being acquired, their value can be determined only by estimation. As mentioned above, the accounting number for these items will be calculated by subtracting the estimated net fair market value of the assets—that is, the fair market value of all identified assets minus all identified liabilities (see Chapters 12 through 14)—from the actual purchase price. This treatment, however, leaves unanswered the question of how much the business is worth, in excess of net asset value. In other words, how much should a purchaser pay for goodwill and going concern value? When a business is put up for sale, the sellers will make an estimate of the value of the business, based largely or totally on estimated future earnings. The business then is priced in one of three ways: (1) at some multiple of projected future earnings (e.g., at five times the estimated annual earnings), (2) at some arbitrary capitalization rate (e.g., one year's earnings divided by 22%), or (3) at the present value of the projected net cash flow for some period of years (e.g., the present value of 10 years' worth of projected cash flows discounted at 15%). The potential purchaser makes similar projections, arriving at an estimated price to pay for the business. The difference between the two estimated values, the seller's and the buyer's, is reconciled by negotiation. The residual between the final price agreed upon and the net asset value estimated by the purchaser is recorded as the value of goodwill. Thus the estimation of a specific value for goodwill is not a distinct goal of the investigation of a potential merger or acquisition. The reliability of the estimate, however, depends on the accuracy and comprehensiveness of the due diligence completed.

Until recently, goodwill could not be deducted against revenues for income tax purposes. As a result, there was no cash flow advantage to amortizing goodwill, and the standard practice was to amortize it across the longest allowed period of time—40 years. The Revenue Reconciliation Act of 1993 changed this provision, allowing an amortization deduction for amortizable Section 197 intangibles, including goodwill, to be taken over a 15-year period, beginning in the month that the intangible asset is acquired. Section 197 intangibles include goodwill, going concern value, franchises (except sports franchises), trademarks, and trade names. Covenants not to compete, copyrights, and patents are also amortizable, but only if they are acquired as part of a purchase of a business. Self-created intangibles are specifically excluded from being amortized.

INTANGIBLE ASSETS DERIVED
FROM TECHNOLOGY

The value of many firms, such as IBM, Intel, and DuPont, is based primarily on proprietary techniques, processes, patents, trademarks, and trade names that were internally developed through extensive high-tech research and development efforts. Products that are so pervasive in our culture that they almost seem part of the natural world, such as nylon, scotch tape, and electronic calculators were all originally developed in the research departments of high-tech firms. Although the patents protecting some of these products have expired, during their life, they made millions of dollars for their owners.

The biggest issue in valuing intangible technological assets, such as patents, is whether or not the patent (trademark, formula, etc.) is defensible. The simple fact of life is that a patent is only as good as the patent holder's ability to sue. Owning a patent does not provide some tangible control over the product, process, or application. It only provides the right to force others to pay royalties for their use. Of course, the patent holder gets to set the price of the license, within bounds. If someone decides to violate the patent rights, the only recourse for the patent holder is to sue. And then, the courts may or may not agree with the patent holder's value for the use of the patent. Additionally, some patents cannot be defended simply because the product, process, or application can easily be duplicated in such a manner that the patent is not violated. Thus the mere existence of a patent does not imply that there is any economic value to its ownership.

The value of patents may be estimated by various methods, depending on the nature of the patent. If the patent is currently being licensed to other businesses, the amount that those businesses are willing to pay is a good indicator of the value of the patent. If the patent has been successfully enforced, as in a prescription drug, an analysis can be made of the current selling price compared to the variable cost of producing the drug. Once the patent expires, other drug companies will begin producing equivalent compounds, and the price advantage will disappear due to competitive forces. The present value of the price differential is approximately the value of owing the patent. The size of the market for the product also has an impact on the value of the patent. A drug that would absolutely reverse male pattern baldness would earn its patent holders billions of dollars—but only if the reverse was temporary, lasting only as long as the drug is used: There is no profit in *curing* a condition, only in *treating* the condition. A drug that would ameliorate the suffering of people with Crohn's disease would be worth a few million, at best. There are hundreds of millions of bald and balding men: There are only a few thousand people with Crohn's disease. As the sales of the marginally effective drug Rogaine demonstrate, millions of bald men will pay, and continue to pay, significant amounts of money to grow hair on their pates. Crohn's suffers will also pay for relief from suffering, but there are simply too few of them for any drug, no matter how effective, to make large amounts of money. Finally, if the patent, process, or application does not have any licensees, does not provide any identifiable price advantage, or has a limited market, the best way to assign a value to the rights is by obtaining expert advice. One may retain an objective engineer or patent lawyer versed in the area to examine the patent and to provide an appraisal of its economic value.

INTANGIBLE ASSETS DERIVED
FROM BUSINESS PROCESSES

Just as many high-tech firms derive their value primarily from the results of research and development, many consumer firms derive their value primarily from assets developed through the process of doing business. Such commercial intangibles include customer recognition, product brands, trade names, customer lists, customer loyalty, databases, telephone listings, reputation, and the skill and expertise of employees. How does McDonald's give you a break today that no other purveyor of hamburgers can? If Coca-Cola is the real thing, is the local store brand cola some kind of fake drink? Does United fly in different, more friendly skies than any other airline? The point is that every reader will immediately recognize all three of these references, and that recognition is a commercial intangible asset that has been proven to be of great value. Name recognition alone is considered to be worth millions of dollars. As was discussed above, a start-up airline recently paid more than a million dollars cash for the rights to use the name *Pan Am*. Its value lies in the immediate recognition of the name by consumers. Who in the United States or Europe has not heard of McDonald's? There is even one on the Champs-Élysées in Paris! The McDonald's name recognition is worth untold millions of dollars, and the company spends additional millions each year to maintain its recognition, and thus its value.

Unlike technological intangibles, the difficulty with valuing commercial intangible assets is that one cannot separate the intangible from the underlying business and evaluate its cash flow effects. Although there is no doubt that the name recognition of McDonald's, Coca-Cola, and United Airlines is very, very valuable, no method exists to explicitly measure that value. The same is true for less well-known business names. A firm that has been successful in business for a long time probably has value in commercial intangibles, such as name recognition and customer loyalty. The problem for a purchaser of that business is how to estimate that value. As with goodwill and going concern value, the process is one of making reasonable assumptions and projecting the cash flow effects based on those assumptions.

One method used to analyze the value of name recognition or customer loyalty is to conduct a survey of current and potential customers. Such surveys are difficult to structure and perform, especially under the time constraints to which due diligence is usually subject. The decision whether to conduct a market survey oneself or to hire a consulting firm to perform the survey should be based on how material the value of the intangible is likely to be and on how extensive the survey must be to provide reliable results. If the business being considered is a machine shop that provides subassemblies to only a few customers, a formal survey is a waste of time and money; simply interview each major customer. If, however, the business is manufacturing and selling consumer products to thousands of customers, a formal market survey may well be the only reasonable means of obtaining the necessary information. If a market survey is being conducted, as discussed in Chapter 4, questions about name recognition and customer perceptions can be included at little added cost.

CONCLUSIONS

The identification, substantiation, and valuation of intangible assets are critical to the investigation of a potential merger or acquisition. Intangible assets, especially of internally produced intangibles, can be the most valuable portion of the firm. However, the process of identifying such assets, substantiating the rights held, and placing a value on intangibles is highly problematic. The most rigorous method of valuing intangibles is to calculate the present value of their future cash flows. Projecting future cash flows, however, involves making numerous assumptions under conditions of great uncertainty. Because of this, the value derived often seems objective and certain when, in fact, it is little better than an educated guess.

The valuing of intangible assets provides a great deal of latitude during the negotiation process. The sellers, while desiring the highest possible price, have the same difficulties in ascertaining the value as do the buyers, but the buyers have a much greater motivation to do a thorough job of evaluating the intangibles than do the sellers. All that the sellers risk is that they might accept less for the business than its maximum value. The buyers risk that they may pay too much for the business ever to return the invested capital and make a business profit. Thus it is likely that the buyers will develop a more accurate estimate of the actual value of the intangibles than will the sellers, providing a negotiating advantage to the buyers. Because of the many assumptions and estimates involved in valuing intangibles, the values derived by sellers and buyers are usually widely divergent. The difference in value assigned provides an area in which compromise can be made, enabling the buyers and sellers to reach agreement.

SUGGESTED READINGS

Brockington, R. (1996). *Accounting for intangible assets: A new perspective on the true and fair view.* Reading, MA: Addison-Wesley.

Donaldson, T. H. (1992). *The treatment of intangibles: A banker's view.* New York: St. Martin's.

Mendell, R. L. (1994). *How to do financial asset investigations: A practical guide for private investigators, collections personnel, and asset recovery specialists.* Springfield, IL: Charles C Thomas.

12 | Short-Term Liabilities

In July of 1987, Norman Brodsky was a rich man. His 50% share of CitiPostal, Inc., was worth more than $20 million. A scant year later, Brodsky was broke. A creditor had seized every penny of his personal bank account. CitiPostal was in bankruptcy. Brodsky's equity was worth, at best, a mere $100,000. "In building his fast-growing business, Norman Brodsky made only one mistake," wrote Robert Mamis (1989, p. 86). "Unfortunately, it was the one mistake he couldn't afford."

Brodsky's mistake was to complete an unsuitable acquisition. He purchased the failing Sky Courier Network, Inc., a same-day package expediter. Although Sky Courier was grossing some $52 million a year, it showed on its balance sheet $9.3 million in long-term debt and a *negative* $15.3 million working capital account.

But it wasn't the debt disclosed on the balance sheet that "did him in." " 'The balance sheet was tough . . . but not impossible,' " said Brodsky (Mamis, 1989, p. 78). What led to disaster were millions of dollars in undisclosed liabilities that Brodsky assumed with the purchase of Sky Courier. As was the case with Automatic Door Specialists, Inc., Brodsky allowed enthusiasm to overwhelm good sense in making an acquisition.

" 'I have to question my own ability to do due diligence,' " Brodsky today confesses in his popular lecture (Mamis, 1989, p. 79).

Many of the undisclosed liabilities that led to the ultimate bankruptcy were short-term liabilities that should have been discovered during the process of due diligence. One can only wonder why they were not. According to Mamis, the extent of the liabilities was missed even by the "Big Eight" accountants. To understand how Brodsky and his accountants

116

were able to miss critical items during due diligence, one must understand the nature of liabilities, especially short-term liabilities.

THE NATURE OF SHORT-TERM LIABILITIES

Short-term liabilities are the converse of short-term assets. Short-term liabilities are business debts that will be due within one year or one business operating cycle, whichever is longer. Examples of short-term liabilities include goods and services purchased on account, taxes payable, and loan payments due within one year. As with short-term assets, the problem for the investigation of a business for merger or acquisition is to determine (a) the existence of short-term liabilities, (b) the amount of their *current* economic value, (c) the characteristics of the obligations in money, services, or product, and (d) the dates at which payments must be made, services rendered, or products delivered to satisfy the terms of the liabilities.

DETERMINING THE EXISTENCE
OF SHORT-TERM LIABILITIES

When investigating a business as a potential acquisition, one attempts to determine the net value of the business. Liabilities are *enforceable* claims that require the future transfer or use of assets or services of the business. Thus liabilities are, in effect, negative amounts that must be subtracted from assets to determine net value.

Accounting rules require that all liabilities be recognized and disclosed on the firm's financial statements, specifically on the balance sheet. However, one of the ways management can "pump up the books" is by misrepresenting the existence, amounts, and timing of liabilities. Management can use the recognition and reporting of short-term liabilities either to make the firm seem to be more profitable and financially sound than it actually is, or to extract cash from the business. The first practice is called *income manipulation*. Although the practice is certainly unethical, and possibly illegal, it is common in businesses being offered for sale. Management often greatly increases currently reported profits by inappropriately shifting expenses to future periods through a manipulation of the characterization and recognition of short-term liabilities. Some examples of increasing current profits (at the expense of future profits, after the business is sold!) are (a) delaying the recognition of transactions that create liabilities, (b) incorrectly identifying refundable advances and deposits received as current revenue, (c) recording as current revenue money collected in advance for services or product, and (d) failing to accrue liabilities for expenses that will be paid in future reporting periods, such as taxes payable after the close of the accounting year. The second practice, extracting additional money from the business, is accomplished by creating false liabilities that will be paid to the current managers or their agents, or by inflating the amounts of actual liabilities and receiving kickbacks when the liabilities are paid.

In Brodsky's case, virtually all of these manipulations went undetected during the due diligence investigation of Sky Courier. Mamis (1989) identifies the following specific examples:

1. $750,000 of withholding and other payroll taxes was not recorded as payables.
2. Rent on the company's buildings was unpaid.
3. The telephone bills were unpaid.
4. $11.9 million of accounts payable were not recorded.
5. $2 million of notes payable had not been recognized on the books.
6. More than $1.2 million was owed to just two airlines.
7. Commissions were paid on future revenues from sales made by people no longer employed at the business.

It is no wonder that CitiPostal went bankrupt after acquiring Sky Couriers. The only wonder is that it managed to hang on for nearly a year before doing so.

As the CitiPostal experience illustrates, a due diligence investigation of liabilities is looking for three conflicting conditions: (1) enforceable obligations that have *not* been recognized and reported, (2) enforceable obligations that have been recognized and reported at incorrect amounts and terms, and (3) amounts that have been recognized and reported, but do *not* represent enforceable obligations of the business.

The process of investigation is essentially the same as that performed by auditors: Extract samples of billings, shipment records, vendors, creditors, and reported liabilities, and trace all of them throughout the accounting system, confirming with independent sources the amounts, timing, and characteristics of each. One obvious source of expert assistance is an auditing firm that is familiar with the industry being investigated. Obtaining the services of a CPA firm is especially recommended when the business being considered has not been subject to a full audit.

In addition to examining the internal records of the business, a search of external sources must be made. A Uniform Commercial Code (UCC) filing search should be made under the official name of the business, any doing-business-as (DBA) names used by the business, and the names of the principal shareholders and the officers of the business. In response to this search, the filing office of the state in which the business is located will produce a listing of all recorded UCC filings, which will show all security interests that have been granted with respect to any assets, any secured borrowings, accounts receivable factoring agreements, and capital leases. Unsecured borrowings will not be listed, as they are not subject to UCC filing.

Other external sources to be examined include a search of public court records and a review of tax returns.

COMMONLY MANIPULATED
SHORT-TERM LIABILITIES

Trade accounts payable and taxes payable are the most commonly manipulated short-term liabilities. Neither liability is subject to third-party recording. Trade payables are evidenced solely by purchase orders and invoices, which can easily be "mislaid." Taxes payable are revealed only by the internal records of the firm. The IRS does not know how much taxes are due (or even if taxes are due) until the firm makes the required filings. It is incredibly easy for management to "put off" both filing tax returns and paying the required taxes. The specific techniques used to examine these two important accounts are discussed below.

Trade Accounts Payable

Trade accounts are obligations that arise from the normal continuing operations of the business, such as purchases of raw materials, merchandise, supplies, and services. The questions to be answered during investigation are, first, is the liability legitimate? That is, does it represent the actual amount and terms of business obligations? Second, are there obligations for purchases that have not been recognized as liabilities?

The method of investigating trade accounts payable is similar to that of accounts receivable. A sample of accounts is taken, including (a) all significantly large accounts, (b) any accounts for which monthly statements are not available, (c) accounts with unusual transactions or terms, (d) accounts with parent or subsidiary businesses, and (e) accounts that have zero balances with major suppliers. The amount owed, the characteristics of the debt, and the payment dates are then all confirmed with the vendors from whom the purchases were made. The purpose of the investigation is to find both improper accounts "owed" to parties related to owners or managers and unrecorded liabilities for accounts payable. It generally is not necessary to contact all the vendors who are owed: Owners and managers are unlikely to be able to obtain kickbacks from large, reputable suppliers. Managers are also unlikely to attempt to extract money through numerous small accounts, because the sheer number of accounts greatly increases the probability of the fraud being detected. The confirmation of zero-balance accounts is one check for unrecorded liabilities.

Several analytical measures can be applied to accounts payable records to disclose the probable existence of improper and unrecorded liabilities. Lists should be prepared, going back at least three years, of the vendors, with purchase amounts and dates, of shipment and receiving dates, and of payment dates. These lists can then be examined to identify any vendors from whom the business does not ordinarily make purchases. It is possible that purchases from new vendors do not actually exist, were made because of a bribe or kickback to the purchasing agent, or were made because of some improper relationship between vendor and purchasing agent. The current amounts of purchases and the amounts owed can be compared to that of earlier years. Finally, any amount showing as past due should be compared with corresponding data for prior years. Various ratios can be compared across years, such as the ratio of gross sales to purchases and the ratio of cash discounts earned to total purchases. Any significant decrease in these ratios may indicate poor management allowing overpurchasing, failure to take discounts allowed, changes in purchase terms by the vendors, or fraudulent manipulation. The pattern of purchases should also be examined by calculating the time between orders and the time between receipt and payment. Significant changes, such as a shift from a few sizable orders to many small orders or an increase in the time between receipt and shipment, may indicate not only unrecorded liabilities, but also problems with the cash flow of the firm.

Finally, a search for unrecorded liabilities includes examining all currently held invoices, vouchers, and canceled checks received after the date of the financial statements provided by the management of the business. One way to manipulate income is to push liabilities into the accounting periods following the end of the accounting year for which the financial statements are being prepared. Inspection of invoices, vouchers, and canceled checks may disclose purchases, transfers, and payments that should have been recorded as liabilities in the prior accounting periods.

Such a push of liabilities can significantly alter reported profits, especially when the purchase item is sizable in amount. An example would be a sign company that received and used steel in the current accounting period. The invoice is "mislaid" or otherwise recorded after the end of the accounting period. In fact, the cost of steel correctly belongs in the prior period, and, if appropriately recorded, it will reduce reported profits of that period by the amount of the invoice received. It is important to trace vouchers and canceled checks to the associated invoices in order to ascertain that the expenses were recorded in the correct accounting periods.

Taxes Payable

Taxes, including federal and state income taxes, as well as sales and property taxes, are material factors in determining both net income and the financial condition of the firm. For a sizable firm that is producing adequate profits, the effective tax rate for all business taxes combined exceeds 50% of gross taxable income. Exacerbating the business problems of confiscatory tax rates is the extremely complicated provisions, calculations, and forms required by the several taxing entities. Thus the calculation and payment of taxes is one area in which both error and fraud commonly occur.

Income Taxes. The level of complexity of federal income tax is affected by the form of entity doing business. Sole proprietorships, partnerships, S corporations, and limited liability companies do not pay taxes. All income from these forms of business is imputed to the owner or partners, who pay taxes on their proportionate shares of the business's profits or losses. C corporations are legal entities that exist separately from their owners, that is, from their stockholders. As legal entities, C corporations pay taxes on corporate profits, without regard to the tax situation of owners.

Corporations usually experience differences between the taxes due on income and the taxes actually paid because of temporary differences between accounting income and taxable income. The difference is carried on the liability section of the balance sheet under the category *Deferred Income Taxes.* It is the liability, *Income Taxes Payable,* that is of immediate interest in investigating a business. The investigation of income taxes payable should include (a) determining the date to which income tax returns have been examined by the IRS, (b) the exact terms and conditions of any disputed amounts or additional assessments made by the IRS, (c) examining at least the three most recent tax returns for completeness and reasonableness, and (d) tracing all amounts in the taxes payable account to income tax returns, paid checks, and other supporting documents.

Employee Withholdings. Employers are required to withhold from employees' wages or salaries amounts for the estimated federal and state income taxes and for FICA, or social security and Medicare/Medicaid taxes. In addition to the withholding amounts, employers are required to pay additional taxes for FICA, equal to the employees' withholding, and for FUTA, unemployment compensation taxes, which varies among industries, businesses, and locales. Most employers are required to make biweekly or monthly deposits of withholdings and employment taxes, and to prepare and file quarterly withholding tax returns.

Despite the politically sensitive nature of the calculation and payment of withholding taxes, and their extreme exposure to IRS audit, it is not at all uncommon for managers and owners of small businesses to fail to file and pay the required taxes, either because of carelessness or a lack of cash flow. Failure to pay required withholdings is a sure path to forced bankruptcy and prison. It is essential, especially when purchasing a C corporation, to be certain that all required withholding forms and taxes have been paid through the date of purchase. Because of the IRS's ability to collect from any "responsible persons," purchase of the business will almost certainly transfer to the new owners the responsibility for any unpaid amounts, including potentially substantial penalties and interest.

Of special concern to purchasers of a business is the issue of independent contractors. Many businesses attempt to avoid paying FICA, FUTA, and withholding taxes by characterizing employees as independent contractors. This issue has been a focus of IRS audits for the last several years. However, because of the low overall rate of audits performed, it is likely that any given business may have gotten away with the practice. As with general withholding, the IRS has the power to collect from any responsible persons. New owners of the business could well find themselves paying huge amounts for withholding, penalties, and interest avoided by the prior owners.

As with income taxes, the investigation technique is to confirm independently the amount of salaries and wages paid by the firm over each of several prior years. The amounts of withholding calculated should then (a) be compared with the filings and payments of all years *not* yet examined by the IRS, (b) be compared with prior years for reasonableness and completeness, and (c) be traced to canceled checks, wire transfers, or other externally prepared documents. Finally, the exact duties and periods worked by all independent contractors should be examined to determine the appropriateness of the classification.

Sales Taxes Payable. In states where sales taxes are imposed, the amounts represent significant expenses for retail businesses. Although the business does not technically *owe* the tax because it is collected from customers as an addition to sales price, the result is that significant amounts of money must be paid to the taxing agency. All retail receipts—both the sales price of the merchandise and any sales tax collected—are deposited into the same cash registers and bank accounts. The moneys are commingled until such time as cash transfers are made to the tax agency. As a result, there are opportunities for management to misrepresent the amount of sales tax due or simply to fail to file and pay the appropriate amount. It should be noted that sales taxes can be a significant, material amount: In some states and localities, the combined state and local sales tax exceeds 10% of gross sales.

Investigation of payable sales taxes should be relatively simple. Because they are trying to sell the business, management most likely will be trying to show the greatest possible sales and profit during the investigation process. The appropriate sales tax rate can be applied to the gross sales amount to derive a close estimate of the amount of tax that should have been reported and paid. The sales tax payable account can then be traced to canceled checks, wire transfers, drafts, or other externally created documentation, and the amounts compared to the estimate. As with income taxes, one should ascertain that any disputes with or additional amounts imposed by the taxing agency have been resolved.

Property Taxes. The last direct business tax that has a material effect is property tax. All fifty states levy and collect some form of taxes on the value of a business's land and buildings, known as its *real property.* Some states also tax business *personality,* that is the property, other than buildings and land, held by the firm. The property tax rates vary widely among states, and are highest in states that have no income tax, such as Texas and Florida. Usually, a business pays property taxes only once a year, and makes a single payment for all property held within the taxing area.

The danger of unpaid property taxes to prospective purchasers is twofold. First, one may become liable for unpaid taxes upon purchasing the business. Second, the business could actually lose title to the property were it to be seized and sold by the state for the back taxes. Either possibility can prove very expensive.

Investigating property taxes payable is straightforward. First, make a list of all taxable property owned by the business. Next, examine all original documents, including assessment forms from the taxing agency, tax bills, canceled checks, transfers, and other documentation; then trace all the documentation to the accounting entries, ensuring that the taxes have been paid and accruals for property taxes are current.

SHORT-TERM BORROWINGS
AND BANK RELATIONS

All businesses, small and large, exist with constant cash flow problems. Rarely do cash inflows from operations ever match cash outflows with exactitude. Invariably, cash inflow occurs infrequently, but in large amounts, while outflows are regular, but in small amounts; or vice versa, depending on the business. This mismatch in timing between cash inflows and outflows makes it impossible to operate without keeping a close working relationship with an experienced banker. Managing cash needs usually requires that a regular source of short-term borrowing be maintained.

It is necessary, in investigating a business for acquisition, to examine the agreements with the business's bank to provide revolving credit or letters of credit. One not only should question what the terms of the revolving credit are, including borrowing limits, repayment requirements, and interest rates, but should also know what supporting documentation the bank requires to substantiate credit worthiness. Furthermore, one should ask if there are limits on such things as total debt, debt to equity ratio, or gross sales. Finally, the prospective buyer should ask if the credit arrangement is transferable. If it is not, then the new owner will be faced with the task of replacing the credit arrangement. In many cases, revolving credit arrangements are either callable on demand, or are callable upon any material change of ownership. Such provisions exist to limit, for the bank, the risk of loss due to the bankruptcy of the business, but they also complicate the task of those who would purchase the business.

To complete the examination of short-term borrowing arrangements, the history of the business's borrowings for at least the past three years should be extracted from the accounting records. The report should include the dates of borrowing, the amount borrowed, the interest rate, and the dates and amounts of interest and principal payments. The record must be evaluated for consistency with the terms of the credit arrangement.

Management should provide a letter of release, allowing the bank officer who handles the business's banking needs to speak candidly with the prospective purchaser or with the purchaser's agent. Often, bankers are less comfortable making disclosures directly to the purchaser than they are to professional agents: other bankers, accountants, or lawyers. Regardless, the banker needs to be appraised of the impending transfer of ownership and provided such information as will allow a decision concerning the terms under which the bank will do business with the new owners.

SHAREHOLDER AND FAMILY MEMBER LOANS

One area subject to significant abuse by the owners of small and closely held businesses is making loans from the shareholders and family members to the business. Often such loans are completely appropriate:

They are a way to put temporary capital into the business or to meet short-term cash flow shortages. Occasionally, however, the loans are fraudulent or are made at terms highly unfavorable to the business. The task of investigating the business for acquisition requires that all such loans be examined in detail. Does the loan represent a true cash infusion into the business? Are the terms of the loan, repayment schedules, and interest rates consistent with market rate loans? Are the loans guaranteed with any business collateral having value in excess of the principal of the loan? Are the loans subject to prepayment penalties or exclusion?

One way in which loans from stockholders and family members are subject to abuse is that the loans may be payments for services rendered, not for cash contributed. Payments for services must, by legislation, code, and regulation, be characterized as compensation, and so be subject to income tax. If the payments can be characterized as a repayment of capital, then only the portion of the payments that represent interest is taxable. The tax savings can be significant. When a business is purchased through stock purchase, all obligations of the corporation, including tax deficiencies, remain with the business. New owners may find the corporation paying substantial taxes, penalties, and interest on transactions that occurred prior to purchase.

A second manner in which such loans may be abused is to make the loans at terms favorable to the stockholder, but unfavorable to the business. Loans may be made at over-market rates of interest, thus transferring business funds to the maker of the loan. The loans may be secured with property that is essential to the operation of the business, and that has a sale or disposal value far in excess of the principal of the loan. The loans may require large, frequent repayments, or be written to provide priority over other obligations in the event of bankruptcy.

In the event that the loans are unfavorable to the business in any way, new owners may desire to retire the loans. If the loans contain any provisions that would make their early payment expensive or that prohibit it, then changing the terms of the loan must be part of the purchase negotiation.

CONCLUSIONS

Short-term liabilities must be carefully investigated during the due process procedure, as they provide several avenues by which management may manipulate income or extract money from the firm. Even if all short-term liabilities are disclosed, are appropriate business obligations, and are at competitive market rates, they represent enforceable demands on the business that must be met within a year. The effects of such obligations on the conduct of business, cash flows, and immediate profitability must be carefully considered in establishing the value of the business as a merger or acquisition candidate.

SUGGESTED READING

Rittenberg, L. E., & Schwieger, B. J. (1994). *Auditing: Concepts for a changing environment.* Fort Worth, TX: Dryden Press.

13 | Long-Term Liabilities

In 1992, Midcom Communications, Inc., a switchless reseller of long distance services, began an aggressive program of acquisitions, purchasing seven companies in two years. In 1992, the company reported $23 million in gross revenues. Two years later, in 1994, gross revenues were reported at $100 million, an increase of over 325%. Stock prices followed the explosive expansion, peaking at nearly $20.00 per share.

On March 4, 1996, shares in Midcom tanked, closing that day at $8.00, a one-day loss of 42%, and a total loss of 60% from the company's peak value. In 1997, a group of dissatisfied investors filed a class action lawsuit against Midcom Communications, alleging, among other things, that management had misrepresented long-term liabilities by improperly reversing amounts for accrued employee benefits and for taxes payable (Stanford University, 1998).

Such a manipulation of long-term liabilities is unusual. Normally, long-term liabilities are the area of business reporting in which interested parties may have the greatest confidence. This is because long-term liabilities are substantiated with written documents and are usually obligations made to parties outside the business. Furthermore, the documents that define long-term liabilities usually are filed with government agencies, and thus are a matter of public record and may easily be examined.

Despite their relative safety, long-term liabilities can be a place where managers misstate the operations and valuations of the business being considered. The process of investigating long-term liabilities is essentially identical to that used to examine short-term liabilities.

THE NATURE OF LONG-TERM LIABILITIES

Long-term liabilities are legally enforceable obligations of a business to transfer assets or services to specified entities at a determined date that falls beyond one year from the current balance sheet date. Examples of long-term liabilities include mortgage loans for real estate, bonds payable, capital leases, multi-year construction projects, and employee retirement benefits.

All enforceable long-term liabilities are subject to the terms of written contracts that specify the obligations and rights of two parties: the lender and the borrower. In all cases, the obligation represents a liability to the borrower. Thus the investigation process primarily consists of obtaining the original contract, examining it to determine its characteristics, and confirming the provisions with the creditor. The items of interest to the investigation are (a) the interest rate of the debt, (b) the term of the debt—that is, the length of time the obligation exists, (c) the date, or dates, and the amount of the payments that must be made, (d) the nature and value of any assets pledged as collateral, (e) the nature of any personal guarantees made, and (f) any restrictions on the borrowing company.

Employee retirement and postretirement benefits, too, are created and substantiated by written documents. Ascertaining the amounts and timing of the payouts of the liabilities, however, is problematic. Retirement benefits depend both on unknown future events, such as the longevity and health of retirees, and on elements that affect the valuation of other long-term liabilities. The entire issue of determining a company's liability for employee benefits is one of ongoing controversy and is far beyond the scope of this book.

The methods and techniques of estimating liabilities for employee benefits, retirement benefits, and postretirement benefits are relatively new topics in business literature. Because of the newness of and small audience for the topic, no popular books or textbooks deal directly and specifically with the issues. There is, however, a sizable body of esoteric publications, intended primarily for lawyers and accountants, which, despite the turgidity of the writing, might be helpful (see Hefty, 1990; Insight, 1994; Dankner, 1981).

Despite the lack of accessible literature discussing the issue, liabilities for employee benefits cannot be ignored, as the potential impact on future earnings can be catastrophic. In 1991, the *Wall Street Journal* reported that IBM, General Electric, and Lockheed had liabilities for postretirement benefits that reduced pretax profits by $2.3 billion, $2.7 billion, and $1.0 billion, respectively (Hooper & Berton, 1991). Although it is unlikely that any entrepreneurial firm being considered for acquisition will have liabilities approaching these amounts, the relative effect of such liabilities can be material to the value of the firm. The best advice for investigating employee benefits is this: If the company being examined has commitments for future retirement and postretirement benefits, obtain the services of an experienced consultant, such as a "Big Six" accounting firm, to estimate the amounts and timing of the liability.

Interest Rates

All long-term liabilities are subject to accumulating interest. Usually the interest charged is specified clearly within the liability instrument as a percentage rate. There are, however, several exceptions to this rule. Occasionally, a long-term liability is created that does not specify an interest rate. In this case, interest is imputed or assumed to be included in the cash payments at current market rates of interest for similar loans or obligations. Often, an interest rate is stated, but is unrealistic: That is, the stated rate is either much greater or much less than the current market rate for similar liabilities. Unrealistic interest rates are commonly encountered in loans from the business to owners, and in loans from the owners to the business. Both cases provide means for owners to extract money from the business in a tax-advantageous manner. One problem with the corporate form of business organization is that money transferred from the business to the owners (i.e., the shareholders) of the business is often taxed twice: once as profits of the business, and once as dividend income for the owners.

Both liabilities that do not specify an interest rate and liabilities that have unrealistic interest rates must be restated. The value of the principal and the amount of interest are recalculated, using present value calculations, to reflect the current market rate. A purchaser of a business will not immediately benefit from misstating interest. In fact, a purchaser often must replace insider notes with new capital, either as equity investment or as new loans. Either way, the true cost of capital must be known to establish the value of the business.

A final exception to a single, stated interest rate is variable-rate notes, also called floating-rate or adjustable-rate notes. Contracts are often made that have interest rates that change with some event external to the business, such as changes in prime rates or changes in the rate for U.S. bonds. Variable-rate loans are generally much riskier for the borrower: Although the borrower benefits from lower rates when the loan is made, there is no protection from increasing rates across the term of the loan.

Long-term liabilities must be examined to determine the contracted or stated interest rate. The contract rate must then be compared with current market rates. If an interest rate is not stated, or if it is unrealistic, then the rate should be restated to show the current value of the principal of the liability and the correct effective interest rate being paid.

The Term of the Liability

The time for which the liability exists is specified in the contract that establishes the obligation. In some contracts, such as mortgages, the term is specified as a number of years or months. Often, however, the term is not explicitly stated; instead, a number of required payments is specified, such as, "360 payments are to be made, beginning on July 1, 1998, and on the first of each month following. . . ." Obviously, it is a trivial matter to determine the remaining term of such contracts. Commonly in long-term bond contracts no term or number of payments is specified, but a specific future date on which the bond matures—that is, the date on which payment is required to be made—is stated. From the point of view of a purchaser of the business, the term is simply the time that will elapse between purchase of the business and the maturity date.

Payment Dates

The date, or dates, on which payments must be made—or assets transferred, or services rendered—are also specified in the liability contract. In the case of loans and bonds, the payments may consist solely of interest or principal, or may combine interest and principal. When assets must be transferred or services rendered, in addition to a specified payment date, a monetary penalty either for being late or for nonperformance is usually stated.

It is essential that the term and payment dates be known, because all liabilities of identical term and stated interest are not equal. As every successful businessperson understands, a dollar today is more valuable than is the promise of a dollar a year from now. One can pay a dollar a year from now by depositing 91 cents in a savings account earning 10% interest. At the end of a year, the account would hold $1—the 91 cents principal plus 9 cents interest earned. This simple concept can be expanded into the calculation of the present value of any pattern of cash flows. Any introductory finance or managerial accounting textbook will include an extensive discussion of present value calculations. Here, it is sufficient to point out that the more frequently interest and principal payments are made, the greater the present value of the loan is, at any stated rate of interest.

For example, consider two corporate bonds, each with a $1,000 face value or principal, each paying 10% interest, and each maturing in 20 years. One bond, *bond coupon,* pays interest of $50 each six months, for a total of 40 interest payments, and pays back the principal at the end of the 20th year. The sum of payments received is $3,000 ([40 × $50] + $1,000). The other bond, *bond zero,* pays nothing for 20 years, then pays the total accumulated interest and principal of $3,000 at the end of the 20th year. *Bond coupon* has a present value of $935, and *bond zero* has a present value of only $446. This concept can be confirmed by examining the *Wall Street Journal* bond quotes. Zero coupon bonds, which pay only upon maturity, are priced at a fraction of the price of an otherwise identical coupon bond, which pays interest semiannually.

Collateral

Collateral consists of assets that are pledged to assure that payment is made when it is due. If the required payment is not made, the creditor has the legal right to seize the collateral in lieu of the payment. Depending on the nature of the collateral and the terms of the debt contract, the debtor may or may not be required to sell the collateral. If the value of the collateral is less than the unpaid payment, then the debtor usually has a right to a general claim against the remaining assets of the business.

The investigation of long-term liabilities includes (a) determining the *exact* nature of all assets pledged as collateral, (b) appraising the current value of all property pledged as collateral, (c) evaluating the importance of the pledged assets to the continuing operations of the business, and

(d) understanding the conditions under which the collateral can be seized and what rights (if any) the business retains in the event of default on the obligation.

Guarantees

Commonly, lenders or business creditors will demand that the owners of small and closely held businesses *guarantee* obligations of the firm. This simply means that the creditor has the legal right to extract payment from the owners or other guarantors in the event that the business fails to meet the obligation. Norman Brodsky's creditor was able to seize Brodsky's personal bank account because of a loan guarantee (Mamis, 1989). Although personal guarantees do not transfer with the sale of a business, the creditor may have the right to demand full payment on transfer, absent the new owner making a similar provision.

If any of the obligations of the firm are guaranteed, the existence and terms of the guarantee should be fully disclosed. Of particular interest to a new buyer of the business is whether the business has offered a guarantee or general obligation in addition to any specific collateral.

Restrictions

One manner in which creditors may limit the risk of loss is by placing restrictions in the contract that establishes the liability. Common restrictions include prohibiting the payment of any dividends while the obligation exists, maintaining a specified debt-to-equity ratio, maintaining specified collateral assets, and keeping a specified minimum net worth of the business.

Two common restrictions on long-term loans and other long-term liabilities are, first, that the obligation cannot be transferred to any person by the borrower, and second, that the loan or liability can be called, or payment demanded, by the creditor prior to the maturity date of the contract. Callable loans are of more interest to prospective purchasers of the business than are nontransferable loans. Nontransferable loans are the responsibility of the person who made the loan, and because they cannot be legally transferred the purchaser of the business cannot be held responsible for the obligation. Callable loans may be transferable, however, creating an obligation on the purchaser of the business. If the callable loan was considered as part of the financing for the purchase of the loan, having it unexpectedly called by the lender can be, at the least, unpleasant, and, at worst, terminal to the operation of the business.

Restrictions commonly do transfer with the purchase of the business. New owners will therefore be subject to the same terms, conditions, and obligations as the former owners. All specified restrictions must be examined and fully understood prior to purchasing a business. Often such restrictions severely limit the ability of the business to modernize operations, replace obsolete equipment, or enter new lines of business.

COMMON LONG-TERM LIABILITIES

There are four common long-term liabilities of which the prospective buyer should be aware: (1) bonds and notes payable, (2) loans from shareholders, (3) mortgages, and (4) long-term capital leases.

Bonds and Notes Payable

A bond is a legal document that constitutes a formal promise to pay both a specific amount of interest at a specified date or dates, and a specified amount of principal at a specified date in the future. The issuer of a bond—that is, the debtor—prepares a formal bond agreement, called a *bond indenture,* that specifies all the terms of the bond, including interest rate, payment date, and all restrictions to which the business is subject. A note payable is a loan from a lending institution or other individual, evidenced by a loan agreement.

Most small companies do not issue bonds to raise capital. Securities law requires disclosure and registration, which is very expensive and thus renders bond debt uneconomic for all except large, multimillion dollar amounts. Large firms commonly do issue bonds, however, and bond debt is often the largest obligation of such a firm.

Almost all businesses do have loans from banks, insurance companies, or other individuals. The most common loans are chattel loans, used to purchase equipment, such as light trucks, machine tools, or business fixtures, and mortgage loans, used to purchase land and equipment. Both chattel and mortgage loans include liens on the purchased property, which can be repossessed by the lender in the event of default. Other common long-term loans include development loans, used to finance research and development, and general acquisition loans, used to purchase a business itself. These loans are often guaranteed by the Small Business Administration, and are referred to as *SBA loans.*

For a variety of reasons, it is economically advantageous to borrow money as a way to raise capital for the business. Although there are a few businesses that are capitalized solely with equity, this is a rare situation. All long-term loans are evidenced with a contract. The due diligence investigation requires obtaining the original agreement, carefully examining it, and confirming its provisions with the creditor.

Loans from Shareholders

Small and closely held businesses are often financed by taking loans from shareholders. At one time this method was commonly used to equalize the investment of the founding shareholders, who were contributing unlike assets to the start-up firm: One shareholder, for example, might provide solely cash, while another contributed essential machinery or rights to a process or patent. If the contributed asset was of substantially greater value than the amount of cash contributed by the other shareholder, then only an equal amount of equity would be issued, with the difference being issued as a loan from the stockholder. This is much less common today, because the 1989 Revenue Reconciliation Act requires that gain or loss be recognized on contributed assets, if the contributing party receives anything other than stock.

Shareholder loans that are disguised dividend payments are of particular interest when examining a business for acquisition, as we discussed in the section on interest payments. Regardless of the form of the acquisition, if the IRS can characterized it as a purchase of the corporation, the new owners become liable for all past liabilities, including taxes and penalties on the value of any assets improperly removed from the business. As with callable loans, unexpected demands for taxes, interest, and penalties can ruin the new owner's day, even if it does not cause the demise of the business.

As with all liabilities, loans from stockholders must be examined to determine the terms, interest rate, and restrictions of the contract. If the loan is in any way unacceptable, it must be renegotiated prior to purchasing the business.

Mortgages

Mortgages are loans secured by real estate: land and buildings. Mortgages with established lending institutions, such as banks and insurance companies, usually are documented properly and contain only market rate provisions. However, mortgage provisions can contain highly restrictive or unexpected provisions. Prospective purchasers of a business must be alert for floating-rate provisions, the right to call the loan on short notice, restrictions on changing or improving the property, or the right to a share of any appreciation in the value of the mortgaged property. Another common restriction included in mortgages is limitations on or prohibitions against early payment of the mortgage. These restrictions can be especially onerous, because they can prevent the owner from obtaining more favorable, lower interest loans; block the business from disposing of obsolete or inappropriate buildings; or obstruct refinancing of the entire business.

Often mortgages to small and closely held businesses are made by stockholders and related parties. When such insider mortgages exist, they must be carefully examined with a large degree of professional skepticism. As with other loans to stockholders and owners, mortgages are an area subject to abuse. The contracts must be examined carefully and exhaustively for any traps that may affect the ability of the buyers to do business in the future.

Long-Term Capital Leases

The nature of long-term capital leases is discussed at length in Chapter 11. Just as capital leases can represent an asset to the business, they can be liabilities, also. Often, assets of businesses are leased to customers in lieu of sales on account. This is especially true in the sign industry, and in medical and restaurant supply businesses.

When a company provides assets to customers on a lease basis, the original leases must be carefully examined to determine their terms and effects on future business. Of greatest importance is the financial soundness of the leasing businesses. Many a sign company has failed when a critical customer went into bankruptcy, returning a number of customized signs for which there was no other buyer. In these cases, the other lease customers of the sign business often find that (a) they have no title to their advertising signs, (b) the bankruptcy court or creditors of the bankrupt sign company are demanding that the signs be purchased under threat of repossession, and (c) there is no one responsible for maintenance or repair of the signs. Although these issues may not result in loss of either the sign or the business, they will invariably prove expensive to settle.

In examining long-term leases, the prospective buyer must ask (a) what the current market value of the leased asset is, (b) what the financial position of the lessee is, (c) what rights to the leased asset the business retains, (d) what market for the leased asset exists, separate from the lease, (e) what obligations the business retains for the leased asset, and (f) if any person or entity has a claim on or equity interest in the leased property.

CONCLUSIONS

The investigation process for long-term liabilities is essentially the same as for short-term liabilities: All internal documents need to be cross-referenced and traced through the accounting records; searches of external sources, including discussions and disclosures from lending institutions, UCC filings, public records, and tax filings, need to be made; the filings and disclosures of all bond instruments must be carefully reviewed; long-term capital lease contracts must be examined and confirmed with the lease; and the originals of all loan agreements must be obtained and evaluated.

SUGGESTED READING

Harrison, H. S. (1991). *How to screen any property for apparent environmental hazards.* New Haven, CT: H^2 Co.

14 | Contingent Liabilities and Pending Litigation

What do Boeing, Midcom Communications, Novell, VanStar, Einstein Bagel, and America Online all have in common? According to the Class Action Clearinghouse, maintained by Stanford University, all these firms, and 477 other U.S. businesses, are currently the targets of class action lawsuits (Stanford University, 1998).

It is an unfortunate fact that doing business in the United States today will almost certainly result in a lawsuit being filed against the business. The suit may be essentially frivolous, such as a customer who tucks a cup of hot coffee between her legs and then proceeds to drive over a speed bump, splashing hot coffee in her lap, or it may be very serious, even potentially fatal to the business, such as harm done by a spill of some toxic substance. In either case, there is a real possibility that the plaintiff will receive a huge cash award. The woman who burned herself with hot coffee was awarded $1,000,000. Dow Chemical in Bhopal, India, has paid out over one thousand times that amount, and is still being sued.

What can be done about lawsuits and other contingent liabilities, other than prayer and insurance? They cannot be avoided, but the potential harm can be limited through careful preparation, ever-vigilant operations, and exhaustive documentation.

The related issues of contingent liabilities and pending litigation are the most problematic in the investigation of potential acquisitions. The difficulty in evaluating their probable future effects is compounded by the problem of finding potential weaknesses in the first place. Unlike with short- and long-term liabilities, there are no agencies that have the responsibility to collect and maintain information concerning such uncertain events. Often contingent liabilities are disclosed accidentally during other phases of the due diligence process. The potential of pending litigation may be found by listening to intercompany rumors, or by "slips" made by owners or officers during the many meetings that are required by the process of buying a business.

Thus in evaluating contingent liabilities and pending litigation one must examine three areas: First, one must find evidence that such potential problems exist; second, one must estimate the amount, timing, and probability of an unfavorable claim being upheld; and third, one must evaluate the possibility and costs of either avoiding or mitigating the liability.

FINDING CONTINGENT LIABILITIES

As mentioned above, no single source exists to maintain files of contingent liabilities. Nor can one trust that management will disclose all such liabilities on the financial statements. Generally accepted accounting principles require that contingencies be recognized and a liability accrued in the balance sheet only if two conditions are met: if it is judged *probable* that the liability will occur, and if the amount of the loss can be *reasonably estimated.* If the loss cannot be estimated, or if the event is judged to be only *reasonably possible,* then no loss is accrued, although a note is required in the footnotes to the financial statements. Under all other conditions, a note is allowable, but not required.

The problem with these conditions for a potential purchaser of the business is that there is no concrete, quantifiable definition of the terms *probable* and *reasonable.* Management has great discretion in determining if any specific event is either. Given that the seller of a business has an interest in showing the greatest possible value of the business, there is strong motivation to find that a potential problem is not probable. Thus serious potential problems may well be known to the owners and officers, but not disclosed in either the financial statement or in any due diligence meetings.

Some contingent liabilities are so common as to be routine: losses on receivables; warranty claims on products; assessments by government agencies for easements, or for utility repairs and improvements; and losses on disposal of business segments. Each of these can and should be disclosed during the investigation of the relevant business functions and are usually both nonmaterial and consistent across time. The area of product warranty claims can, however, be both material and inconsistent. If the company has recently introduced a new product, has unusually long warranty periods, or has experienced a significant increase in warranty claims recently, then excessive warranty costs may occur in the near future. Consequently, if any of these conditions exist, a full investigation of the causes must be made.

Warranty on products and the manufacturer's liability for the use (and misuse) of products has caused the demise of entire businesses and industries. In the 1980s all manufacturing of small aircraft ceased in the United States. Boeing, Douglas, Beech, Fairchild, and others continued to produce airliners and multi-engine business planes, but no manufacturer made single-engine airplanes. Some businesses that supplied *only blueprints* from which single-engine planes could be built at home went out of business. Eventually, the U.S. Air Force had to purchase primary trainers from Italy! It is only since the mid-1990s, after congress passed legislation limiting the product liability of aircraft manufacturers, that production of single-engine airplanes has resumed.

Thus when a business is being considered for acquisition, it is essential to investigate, carefully and completely, all possible contingent liabilities, not only of the business, but also of the industry of which the business is part.

PENDING LITIGATION

Discovering pending litigation often can be accomplished by a search of public records in the local and state courts in the locales where the company does business. In most states, at least recent records have been entered into computer databases, which can greatly ease and speed the search process. Otherwise, the search includes physically examining printed indexes and following relevant entries to the original court documents. Such searches are best conducted by either lawyers or experienced paralegals who are familiar with the process.

In addition to a search of court records, a search of local newspaper files, of the LEXIS/NEXIS database, and of the indexes of the *Wall Street Journal* and the *New York Times* may well disclose stories that discuss events that may lead to lawsuits. A search of the LEXIS/NEXIS database may also disclose any pending federal litigation. A search of the Class Action Clearinghouse maintained by Stanford University will disclose if such action has been filed against the business or against any business in the industry since December 22, 1995.

The purpose of such searches is threefold: One seeks to find (1) liens and judgments that have not been disclosed on the financial statements; (2) evidence of past and current litigation that names the business, the owners, or the officers as defendants; and (3) information that will allow one to better estimate whether or not lawsuits might be filed in the near future.

To the extent possible, the settlement of each case found should be ascertained. This is often not possible, as cases are often settled by negotiation and both parties are sworn not to reveal the details of the settlement. However, if the suit resulted in a monetary payment by the business, a record of that payment should be in the accounting system. Regardless, the frequency and nature of the cases found will often allow inferences to be drawn concerning the business ethics and practices of the owners, officers, and employees of the business.

EVALUATING THE LIABILITY

Evaluating a business's exposure to either contingent liabilities or pending litigation is a process of making informed judgments, assigning probabilities, and making estimates. In other words, one guesses. Of course, the penalty for guessing wrong can be quite severe, particularly if the guess underestimates the size or seriousness of the event. Unless one either is expert in both the business being investigated and the events that are being considered as potential liabilities, or is so wealthy that the potential loss is of little concern, then the estimate should be made in a "what if" format. The potential damage should be evaluated under a variety of conditions, considering at least, the best-case possibility, the worst-case scenario, and the case judged most likely.

This is certainly an area in which the assistance of outside consultants is appropriate. Lawyers may be able to give reasonable estimates of the probability of a lawsuit being filed, of an unfavorable judgment, and of the probable size of such a judgment. Officers of businesses in the industry may, from experience, be able to make estimates of the frequency and size of unfavorable judgments. Auditors tend to specialize in specific industries and often have specific experience that can be the basis for evaluating the size and probability of contingencies and judgements.

SUGGESTED READING

Alexander Hamilton Institute. (1993). *Legal liability audit.* Ramsay, NJ: Author.

15 | Owner Discretionary Spending

In closely held businesses, the issue of discretionary spending by owner-managers is of serious concern. Small business owners do not like to show profits. Profits are subject to income taxes. If the business is a C corporation, profits get taxed twice: once when earned and again when paid out in the form of dividends. One way to avoid profits and the concomitant taxes, while still enjoying the things that profits can buy, is to spend business revenues on personal use items. This practice is widespread and not limited to "mom and pop" operations. Leona Helmsley spent several months in prison for avoiding income taxes, in part by using hotel revenues to furnish her personal residence. Several other ways exist to reduce reported profits while keeping the benefits of the business's revenues: (a) by paying excessive salaries to owner-managers, (b) by paying "salaries" to family members who do not actually work in the business, or (c) by providing such perks as automobiles, business trips, expense accounts, and corporate credit cards to owners and family members. All of these areas must be examined during the exercise of due diligence in evaluating a merger or acquisition.

OFFICER SALARIES

The owners of a business are often the officers of that business. The question to be answered in performing due diligence is whether or not the officers are worth their compensation. In some cases, the officers will be receiving much more than their ability and efforts deserve; in other cases, much less. One way to evaluate the appropriateness of the compensation package is to compare it with what would be paid if an *outsider,* someone without ownership rights, was employed in the position. This is a valid comparison for two reasons: First, a compensation consistent with the market rate for executives in similar positions represents the economic value of the position; and second, if the business is acquired, the owner-officer most likely will be replaced with a hired manager. Thus the market rate for the executive position represents the most likely future cash flow effect in the event of acquisition or merger.

Information concerning officer compensation can be obtained from a variety of sources: Trade organizations often compile information concerning wages and compensation packages; magazines such as *Forbes* often publish surveys of officer compensation; consultants and placement specialists by necessity compile and maintain information concerning officer compensation; and, finally, the jobs service of the local state employment agency often has comparative compensation statistics. When using these sources, one must be careful to evaluate the companies for which the data is being reported. Most often, data on officer compensation is collected only from the largest businesses in an industry. As such, the reported numbers may not be completely representative of the compensation being paid in smaller firms. The best approach, therefore, is to make an estimate of compensation range, and to be prepared to modify it as information becomes available.

OVER-MARKET OR UNDER-MARKET
EMPLOYEE WAGES AND SALARIES

An issue similar to that of officer salaries is the appropriateness of wages and salaries paid to the employees of the firm. There are situations where employees are overpaid relative to the market for the skills and experience required by the position. There are several reasons why this may occur: (a) the owner-manager may not be aware of what market wages and salaries are; (b) the employee may have received numerous raises over several years; (c) the employee may, in good years, have been given raises, which tend to be permanent, rather than bonuses, which tend to be one-time payments; or (d) the employee may be a close friend of the owner-manager, and the pay discrepancy therefore might be deliberate. Sometimes, the opposite occurs: Employees are underpaid relative to the market for the skills and experience required by the position. The reasons for underpayment are also several: (a) the owner may be unaware of market rates of salaries and wages; (b) the employee may *not* have received appropriate raises during the period of employment; (c) the employee may have chosen to remain employed at below scale compensation rather than suffer the stress of changing jobs; or (d) the employee may have accepted below scale compensation because of friendship and loyalty to the owner-manager.

Both situations are undesirable. Wages that are either too high or too low for the skills and effort of the employee lead to dissatisfaction and lowered productivity (Adams, 1963). Each situation is less than optimal for the business: Overpaid employees are an unnecessary and avoidable cost to the business; underpaid employees tend to be dissatisfied and are likely to leave the business when it changes ownership, causing the avoidable expense of obtaining and training replacements.

As with compensation for officers, statistics of employee compensation may be obtained from a variety of sources, including trade organizations, consultants, the state Jobs Service Office, and the Bureau of Labor Statistics. The compensation of key employees should be determined from the books of the business and then compared to the market rates. If the actual compensation differs substantially from market rates, the causes of the discrepancy should be determined and the potential effect on future business in the event of acquisition carefully evaluated.

FAMILY SALARIES

It is very common in closely held and family run businesses for salaries to be paid to family members who are not working for the business. It is a way to extract money from the business while simultaneously avoiding double taxation and obtaining a lower average family tax rate than would be provided if the money were paid solely to working family members. Such practices are illegal. At best, if detected, the practice will lead to significant tax penalties. At worst, the guilty family members will be required to pay significant fines and will serve time in prison. Sometimes, the family member does work at the business—at least spending normal working hours there—but is so incompetent that the position is nothing more than a sinecure provided to keep peace in the family. The practice is also used as a method to provide health care coverage for adult children and family members who otherwise would not be covered.

It is also common for family members to work in the business, often long hours at difficult jobs, and receive no pay at all. This practice is very common in the restaurant industry, where children and spouses work in the restaurant, but are never put on the books. This has severe implications for a prospective purchaser of the business. If the business is acquired, the nonpaid family members will have to be replaced with paid workers. This will entail significant increases in wages, unemployment and workers' compensation insurance, social security, and Medicare taxes.

Wages paid to family members, whether or not appropriate for the work actually done, should be recorded in the books of the firm. A perusal of the books, as in other areas of investigation, should disclose exact amounts of family member compensation and related benefits. The examination of the books for family compensation must include the petty cash records. Although the amounts are usually small, family members often dip into petty cash in lieu of compensation. Because such payments are not characterized as compensation, there is no withholding made for FICA or income taxes. The total effect, if several family members are engaging in the practice, can be significant.

Thus it is essential to identify all family members working in the business, to evaluate the quality and quantity of work they perform, to determine the exact compensation each is receiving, and to compare that compensation with market rates for the job being done. The appropriate compensation and employee costs then should be used in making business and financial forecasts.

PERKS FOR FAMILY MEMBERS

Another way by which family members are able to avoid taxes on funds extracted from the business is through excessive and inappropriate perquisites. Perquisites, or perks, are amounts paid over and above salary, wages, and typical fringe benefits for items that have value to the individual. An example of a perk is providing first-class airline travel. Although the trip itself may be a business necessity, the cost of first-class travel over the cost of coach represents a perk enjoyed by the individual. Common perks encountered in businesses include company cars, travel and entertainment expenses, personal telephone bills, and services such as yard care, snow removal, and childcare.

The appropriateness of perks is a gray area, and only a careful examination of the business reason for the perk, the cost of the perk, and the availability of alternatives for the perk will reveal if they are suitable or not. Each perk enjoyed by various family members must be identified and separately evaluated to determine its appropriateness to the business under consideration.

Company cars often have a clear business purpose: transportation for such business necessities as sales, contract negotiation, and site inspections. However, it is common that owners and family members are furnished cars that are used for commuting between home and work or for personal needs: Neither of these uses has any business purpose, but the costs are borne by the business, providing a benefit to the individual while allowing both that individual and the business to avoid taxes. The use of company cars can be investigated by examining expense reports and logs of auto usage, and by asking questions of the people using the cars.

The lack of such records should be a red flag. Any company should have records contemporaneous with the expenses that are sufficient to satisfy the requirements of the Internal Revenue Service. As small businesses are high priority audit targets for the IRS, the likelihood that undocumented automobile expenses would be disallowed for tax purposes is quite high. If deductions for automobiles are disallowed because of inadequate records, the IRS simply recalculates the tax due and, if indicated, adds penalties and interest. False records are evidence of an attempt to avoid taxes, which is a crime. Thus if the cost of automobiles is being improperly charged to the business, the risk of punishment is much less if there are no records than if there are fraudulent records.

In the event that adequate records do not exist, the safest course for the exercise of due diligence is to assume that the cost of any automobile being used by a family member is being inappropriately charged to the business. Assume that, as a new owner, the deduction will not be available, and adjust the estimates of taxable income upward by the amount that is currently being deducted.

Company airplanes, like company autos, are often of questionable business use. Even a small four-passenger single-engine airplane can provide much more transportation than many small businesses ever need. The arithmetic is simple: Assume that an airplane is used for four hours each business day. A single-engine airplane, such as a Beechcraft Bonanza, a Cessna 210, or a Mooney Executive, can average close to 170 miles per hour, including time spent getting to and from the runway on the ground. Four hours of use multiplied by 170 miles per hour, multiplied by 4 business passengers, multiplied 250 days of use per year, equals 680,000 seat-miles. If only one person uses the plane at a time, the plane still provides 170,000 miles of travel in a year: the equivalent of 21 round-trip journeys between New York and Los Angeles.

The use and cost of a company airplane must be examined carefully during due diligence for two reasons: First, because there is a high probability that the airplane is an unnecessary luxury preferred by the current owner-manager, and second, because there is a high probability that using a private plane is actually much more expensive than would be equivalent airline fares. The cost of owning and flying a four-passenger single-engine airplane for the number of hours calculated above would approach $100,000. Twenty-one *first-class* round-trip tickets would cost no more than $34,000. The difference between these two costs is the cost of the owner-manager's desire for a private plane. If the airplane cannot be justified as a necessary business expense, then it most likely represents a way in which the business owners or managers are taking tax-free money out of the business.

The investigation of the use and cost of a company plane starts with the company accounting records. These records can be substantiated by cross-checking them with records maintained by the mechanic who performs FAA required annual inspections on the plane. The FAA designated inspector must keep certain records of each aircraft inspected. In addition, each pilot of the plane is supposed to maintain a personal log to substantiate FAA experience requirements. The pilot logs can be examined to determine the date of any flights, their destination, and the names of any passengers carried. As with the investigation of automobile costs, the lack of any of these required records should be considered prima facie evidence of management abuse.

Travel and entertainment is another widely abused perk. The rules that govern the deductibility of these expenses are beyond the scope of this book; however, tax rules require that to be deductible travel must (a) be overnight, and (b) be primarily for a purpose *directly* related to the business. For meal expenses to be deductible, not only must the taxpayer or employee of the taxpayer be present at the meal, but meal expenses must also (a) be directly related to or associated with doing business, and (b) not be lavish or extravagant. Other forms of entertainment, including club dues and ticket expenses for events, may or may not be deductible, depending on the nature of the club, the business purpose of the expense, and various specific limitations in the Internal Revenue Code and Regulations.

Foreign travel is also commonly abused. The owner of a pizza restaurant may well have a clear understanding of the business purpose of a two-week trip to Italy. This understanding may not be shared by the IRS or by any potential purchaser of the business. Specific IRS rules determine both the deductibility and limitations of expenses for foreign travel. The travel must be primarily for business. If the trip is longer than 7 days, or if more than 25% of the time away is spent on personal matters, the expenses *must* be allocated between deductible business costs and nondeductible personal travel expenses. For more information, see the list of IRS publications at the end of this book.

Other perks that may be abused involve personal expenses that are paid by the firm and deducted as business expenses. Such items as personal telephone bills, lawn mowing, snow removal, minor house repairs, and childcare expenses often are inappropriately included in business expenses. If the firm has grounds crews or maintenance personnel who routinely maintain business properties, they may well "swing by the boss's house" while on company pay. The cost involved is rarely material; occasionally, however, as with the Helmsley case, the amounts involved are substantial. Detecting such practices may be quite difficult. One may find evidence by examining expense ledgers, reconciling business expenses to vendor invoices, or asking employees about such practices.

IRS enforcement is such that one may count on the firm having either extensive itemized expense forms or a per diem allowance that is consistent with IRS limitations. Although IRS enforcement is rigorous, many firms have not been subject to an IRS tax audit. If the firm has sizable expenses for travel and entertainment, abuse by owners and family members may well go undetected. Therefore it is necessary that the prospective purchasers make a careful examination of the records of travel and entertainment expenses.

PHILANTHROPIC GIVING

Owners of small businesses are solicited constantly by organizations, large and small, for donations of goods, services, and money. Often such contributions are appropriate to build and maintain goodwill with the community within which the business is located. It is common for restaurants and soft drink bottlers to contribute product to schools, youth groups, and community groups. However, such expenses may not have a clear business purpose and, in fact, may be nothing more than a way for a business owner to support a hobby while simultaneously reducing income taxes. Often such giving is made for the same reasons that nonworking family members are kept on the payroll.

The issue for the purchaser of a business is to gauge whether or not the philanthropic giving is appropriate: Does the giving have a business purpose? Are the amounts such that they do not extract capital needed by the firm? Obviously there is no objective answer to either of these questions. One may only identify the amounts, recipients, and use of the funds, and make a value judgment about just how appropriate the donations are.

CONCLUSIONS

Owners of small or closely held businesses do not like to report profits. Profits mean that income taxes must be paid. If the business is organized as a C corporation, profits may well cause double taxation, once at the corporate rate, and again at the individual rate when dividends are paid. Thus it is common for owners of small businesses to engage in a variety of activities to extract funds from the business in a manner that allows the funds to be characterized as deductible business expenses. These activities range from those that are allowed, or at least are accepted, to those that are clearly illegal.

The issue for the purchaser of a business is to determine the extent to which such activities are used in the business under examination. Funds currently being extracted from the business by the owners become available to purchasers of the business upon transfer of ownership. Thus the amounts, timing, and method of extraction of the funds are of great interest in a potential merger or acquisition.

SUGGESTED READINGS

Edwards, S., & Edwards, P. (1996). *Secrets of self-employment: Surviving and thriving on the ups and downs of being your own boss.* New York: G. P. Putnam's Sons.

Phelan, D. J. (1995). *Success, happiness, independence: Own your own business.* Lakewood, CO: Glenbridge.

16 | Placing a Value on the Business

Once the due diligence investigation is complete, a final, essential question remains to be answered before any acquisition can be finalized:

What is this business worth?

By now, it should be no surprise that there is no one answer to this question. Everyone has an opinion. Ask the seller. Ask your accountant. Ask your lawyer. Ask your banker. Ask your spouse. Each will have an answer: No two answers will agree.

But an answer must be found. If the acquisition is to be completed, the answer must be acceptable to both the buyer and to the seller. Simply reaching an agreement, however, is no guarantee that the answer is correct, that the value agreed upon is the *true* economic value of the firm as an ongoing entity. The business press is replete with stories of businesses sold for too little and businesses bought for too much. In fact, disputes over the value of a business are the basis of most class-action lawsuits that arise from mergers and acquisitions. According to the Class Action Clearinghouse (Stanford University, 1998), nearly 60% of all actions allege that accounting fraud caused the misvaluation of the firm.

Of course, the primary purpose of the due diligence investigation of the firm was to uncover accounting fraud. Suppose that no fraud, misrepresentation, or error exists. The question remains:

What is this business worth?

VALUATION METHODOLOGIES

There are at least six defensible ways to place a value on any business. None is correct: At best, they are all approximations. In the final analysis, the value placed on the business will be the product of a series of guesses—preferably *educated* guesses. The better the guesses, the more likely that the business will be priced correctly: neither so high that the new owners cannot succeed, nor so low that the old owners do not receive fair market value for their business.

1. Owner's Asking Price

Every business for sale has some asking price. This is the price that is either what the owner believes the business is worth or what the owner hopes to get, if some sucker comes along. The owner's asking price may be completely arbitrary, may be based on some economic measure of the business, or may be some stochastic figure, such as a multiple of gross sales.

The most common basis used by owners to establish price is the price received for similar businesses. This concept is identical to the comparable sales approach commonly used to establish value for real estate. Such comparables can be valuable when the business is relatively small and one of many such businesses in the area. Restaurants, bars, tax services, auto repair, and office services are examples of such businesses. The competitive environment, ready market, and easily substantiated revenues and expenses of these businesses make comparable sales both available and reasonable to use for valuation.

For businesses in fields where there are few firms nationwide, such as sign manufacturers, injection plastic molders, or makers of automobile seats, and for larger businesses, comparable sales are not very useful. First, there is unlikely to be a recent sale of a comparable business. Second, if a recent sale exists, it is unlikely to be in the same geographic area. Third, it is unlikely that the business recently sold and the business being valued are actually comparable in size, investment, and cash flow. Thus larger businesses are likely to have asking prices based on the book value of the firm or on some multiple of earnings. Each of these valuation methods is discussed in detail below.

Asking prices are also set by applying various stochastics. For example, it is common for bed and breakfast inns to be priced at either five times the annual gross or ten times the gross profit, before owner draws. In businesses where revenues and costs are reasonably stable across firms, such stochastics can provide reasonable prices. However, such stochastics fail (a) when businesses are highly variable from firm to firm, (b) when there are no revenue or costs features that are common from business to business, or (c) when the business is in a regulated industry.

The owner's asking price cannot be accepted as authoritative. The reality of selling a business is such that every owner "jacks up" the price a little to allow for some compromise with the buyer, while still obtaining the highest price possible for the business. The asking price is likely to be based on the price at which similar businesses have recently traded. If there is no comparable sale on which to base a price, the price is likely either the book value of the firm or some multiple of earnings.

2. Book Value

The book value of a business is simply the net worth of the firm as reported on the balance sheet. Book value is simply the total assets of the business minus total liabilities.

Book value is a good starting point for the purchaser of a business, as it usually understates the economic value of the business. Generally accepted accounting principles (GAAP) require that all assets initially be recorded at the price paid for the asset. (GAAP is actually a little more complicated than this, but this statement is close enough for the purpose here.) The value of the asset is then reduced each accounting period on a regular, systematic basis: a process called *depreciation* or *amortization*. Depreciation methods, which are numerous, are all arbitrary, and only by sheer accident do they ever approximate the true reduction in the value of the asset because of use and age. Further complicating the issue of book value is the fact that some assets do not decline in value, and actually may increase in value over time. Suppose that in 1920 one had purchased the rights to the name *Coca-Cola*. No matter what the 1920 price was, the 1998 price is much, much higher. The book value, however, would be zero or nearly zero, depending on the method by which the asset was amortized.

Book value makes a good starting point for assigning a value to the business, but it should be recognized that the book value is not likely to reflect the economic value, and so appropriate adjustments should be made.

3. Adjusted Book Value

Adjustments are made to book value to better reflect economic value. Appropriate adjustments may either increase or decrease book value. Some assets will be undervalued in the books because depreciation or amortization has exceeded the economic use of the asset. Other assets may well be overvalued because depreciation has understated the change in value of the asset.

Often, the most valuable assets of the business are not reflected in book value at all. This is true of internally produced patents, proprietary processes and techniques, and self-produced trademarks. Thus when adjusting the book value of a business, the value of intangible assets must be added.

Adjustments to the book value may be based on (a) the fair market value of the asset, (b) the realizable value of the asset, or (c) the replacement value of the asset.

The fair market value of an asset is the price that asset would bring in a market with a willing seller and buyer. Short of actually selling the asset, fair market value can never be determined exactly. Thus fair market value must be estimated, usually by a comparison of recent sales of similar assets.

The realizable value is the amount an asset would bring, assuming that it was sold at market value, less the costs of selling. Because realizable value is based on fair market value, it cannot be known with certainty, but must also be estimated.

Replacement cost is the cost that would be incurred in replacing the asset as installed. Thus replacement cost includes acquisition cost, shipping, installation, and set-up. If the asset is of a type that is commonly traded, such as a Caterpillar crawler tractor, the replacement cost can be very closely estimated. If the asset is some custom-built machine or building, estimating replacement cost becomes at least as problematic as estimating fair market value.

The adjusted book value more closely approximates economic value than does book value, because estimates of the value of self-produced intangible assets are added, and because the values of other assets are increased or decreased, as appropriate, to better approximate their market values.

4. Liquidation Value

Liquidation value is the residual amount of money that would remain if the business were shut down, all assets were sold at market value, and all liabilities were paid. Liquidation value, therefore, is useful for sellers, because it can be used to set a "floor" price, below which they would be better off to liquidate the business rather than to sell.

The estimation of liquidation price uses the adjusted book value as a starting point. The realizable value of each asset is separately estimated, assuming some reasonable period in which to dispose of all assets. Assets, such as real estate, can be appraised by experts. The sum of the realizable value is reduced by the total of liabilities, and the remainder is the liquidation value of the business.

5. Multiple of Earnings

A common method employed to place a value on a business is to multiply the annual earnings by some value. Various rules of thumb exist for different businesses. As mentioned above, bed and breakfast inns are commonly valued at ten times their annual earnings, before owner draws. Thus a B & B that was showing a business profit of $50,000 per year would be priced at $500,000. Outdoor sign companies are often priced at six to ten times their earnings. The range of multiples reflects the wide range of asset values typical of the businesses. Some outdoor sign companies have very small assets, because locations, signs, and equipment are all obtained with operating leases. Other companies own their locations, signs, and equipment.

There are several drawbacks to using a multiple of earnings to estimate a business's value. First, the earnings used are the historical earnings, either those of the current year or an average of some number of prior years. Second, using a multiple of earnings does not allow for known current or expected future changes in the business or in the earnings stream. Third, the characteristics of the business will *always* change when the business changes owners. Earnings may well decrease because the purchase is financed, and so the interest increases, or because business is lost due to customers leaving when ownership changes. Finally, the multiple used invariably is based on some industry average return. It is only an accident if the business being valued is "average" within its industry.

6. Discounted Future Earnings

The method favored by business colleges is to use discounted future earnings. In theory, the stream of future earnings is discounted, or di-

Table 16.1 Net Present Value of Cash Flows

	Year 1	Year 2	Year 3	Year 4	Year 5	Total
Cash inflows	$100,000	$110,000	$120,000	$130,000	$140,000	$600,000
Present value @ 15%	$86,957	$83,176	$78,902	$74,328	$69,605	$392,967
Value of the business in today's dollars				$382,967		

vided, by some required rate of return. The resulting quotient is the value of the business. The use of discounted future earnings explicitly recognizes that the value of a business is its *future earnings,* not its past earnings. One need only look to the many failed businesses to understand this concept. What is the value of Osborne Computers, Inc.? Osborne, the first manufacturer of what are now called laptop computers, earned hundreds of millions of dollars during the 1970s and early 1980s. Today, there is no Osborne Computers. Had future earnings been accurately forecast, the company would have had a near zero value.

A simple example of how discounted future earnings works would be if the business under consideration was estimating that it would earn $100,000 next year and that earnings will increase $10,000 per year for the next five years. Assume that the buyer needs to make a 15% return on capital. How much capital can be invested so that the earnings represent a 15% return on capital? In other words, what value does the business have if future earnings are discounted by a rate of 15%? Table 16.1 presents the net present value as determined by this method.

This is an extremely simplified model. It implies that the business can be valued at $392,967. A cash investment of $392,967 will return a total of $600,000 over 5 years, which is the same as investing the $392,967 in a savings account that earns compound interest at 15%. The example above is the same as calculating an internal rate of return of 15%.

Using discounted future earnings or discounted future cash flows is the most commonly taught method in business schools. It is also the method used by investment bankers to establish value. It has one major drawback, however: A discounted future earnings calculation looks scientific, precise, and accurate, but it is none of these things. Future earnings and future cash flows are unknown: Remember Osborne Computers. Future earnings must be estimated. There is simply no reason to believe that the estimate of future cash flows is any more accurate or exact than any other estimates that can be made. Thus the value derived by using discounted future earnings is no more reliable than the assumptions and estimates used to forecast those future earnings.

There is no theoretical method to address this problem. *Estimate* is a Latinate word for *guess*! One more or less accepted method employed to address the shortcomings of discounted future earnings calculations is to assign probabilities to the estimates. This complicates the calculations, but provides a more conservative—read "lower"—valuation. Another approach is to establish ranges of future earnings, assuming worst-case, expected, and best-case projections. None will exactly match what occurs, but if a good enough job is done of making estimates, actual results will be somewhere within the range.

CONCLUSIONS

There is no single way to establish the value of a business. In practice, the value at which a business changes ownership is the result of a bargaining process that balances the seller's desire for the highest possible price with the buyer's desire for the lowest.

To have the strongest possible position for the bargaining, all the valuation methods above should be completed. The differing values derived then should be compared and examined to understand the causes of the differences among them. When one is assured that every approach to valuation has been thoroughly and accurately completed, some average of the values can be calculated. The absolute high price that the buyer is willing to pay and the rock-bottom bargain price that the seller is willing to accept should be determined. Then, and only then, should bargaining begin.

Caveat emptor!

SUGGESTED READINGS

Lipman, F. D. (1996). *How much is your business worth? A step-by-step guide to selling and ensuring the maximum sale value of your business.* Rocklin, CA: Prima.

Robinson, B. R., & Peterson, W. (1995). *Strategic acquisitions: A guide to growing and enhancing the value of your business.* Burr Ridge, IL: Irwin Professional.

IRS Publications

IRS publications are available in print form at most IRS offices and at most public libraries. They also may be downloaded from the IRS web site: http://www.irs.treas.gov/

Publication Number 334. *Tax guide for small businesses.*

Publication Number 463. *Travel, entertainment, gift and car expenses.*

Publication Number 535. *Business expenses.*

Publication Number 552. *Record keeping for individuals.*

Publication Number 583. *Starting a business and keeping records.*

Sources of Demographic Information

The following sources of demographic information can be found on the World Wide Web.

American Demographics (http://www.marketingtools.com/index.htm): This is the home site of American Demographics. It provides many demographic databases and publishes several journals. There is a limited amount of free information.

The Right Site (http://www.easidemographics.com): This site has a large volume of free demographic information, which may be searched and downloaded. It also sells demographic databases on CD ROM and provides research assistance for a fee.

U.S. Department of the Census (http://www.census.gov): There is a limited amount of free demographic information at this site. A $40 three-month subscription fee provides access to statistics of building permits, federal expenditures, survey of manufacturers, census tract street index, business activities, and business statistics nationwide by counties and by zip codes.

Tasks to Be Completed
for Due Diligence

Before due diligence begins, one should accomplish the following things:

1. Obtain copies of the following items:
   a. Articles of incorporation, bylaws, and minutes of the meetings of the board of directors
   b. List of shareholders, number of shares, securities, units, or other forms of ownership
   c. Brochures and advertising materials
   d. Financial statements since start-up
   e. Current-year financial statements, both monthly and quarterly
   f. Annual reports and statements
   g. Any filings with federal and state governments
   h. Organizational charts
   i. All management forecasts of revenues, expenses, and cash flows
2. Identify all items that can be considered extraordinary or nonrecurring.
3. Calculate operating and nonoperating income.

During the due diligence investigation, one should carry out the following:

1. Prepare a corporate organization chart showing the relationship between each owner and each subsidiary, division, joint venture, partnership, or minority interest.

2. Prepare a list of all officers and key employees, their titles, ages, duties, responsibilities, length of service, education, and compensation for the last three years.

3. Obtain copies of the following items:
   a. Any operating permits
   b. All licenses
   c. All consents, orders, authorizations, and decrees from federal and state governments

4. Determine if the business receives any form of subsidy or grant. If so, ascertain what the details are.

5. Obtain listings of all real estate and facilities, and take photographs of each facility. Examine each contract to determine the following:
   a. The address and legal description of the property
   b. The physical description and use of each
   c. The date obtained, price, cost of improvements, estimated market value, current tax basis, and current book value for each property
   d. The date leased, the expiration date of the lease, payments, disposition of improvements, and likelihood of renewing any leases upon maturity
   e. The number of employees at each facility
   f. The size of each property (in feet, meters, hectares, etc.)
   g. The age and condition of each facility
   h. The mortgages, if any, and their amounts, payments, interest rate, and balloons. Remember to compare these amounts to financial statements.
   i. If there are any leases or subleases granted to third parties. If so, obtain copies of them.
   j. The tax appraisals, rates, and due dates
   k. The estimated difficulty of marketing the property if Aerolineas should decide to abandon it

6. Obtain listings of all equipment and ownership details or lease terms for each piece of equipment, as for real estate and facilities. Be especially careful to obtain such information as age, hours of use, and condition to estimate market value.

7. Obtain listings of all spare parts for equipment.

8. Obtain listings of all computers, software, and databases owned, leased or used by the business.

9. Obtain copies of any appraisals done on assets, real estate, facilities, and equipment.

10. Obtain a copy of the marketing plan, if one exists.

Questions to Be Answered During the Exercise of Due Diligence

B usiness Description:

1. What is the legal name of the business?
2. What other legal names, abbreviations, and shortened names are used?
3. What is the legal form of the business?
4. What are the names, telephone numbers, and addresses of the principals involved in negotiating this transaction?
5. What proof is there that these people have legal authority to sell the business?
6. What are the names, telephone numbers, addresses, and percentage ownership of all persons who hold equity in the business?
7. What is the history of the business?
8. What subsidiary businesses are part of the business?
9. What are the divisions of the business? What are the names of all managers, their addresses, and their activities?
10. What joint ventures or partnerships with the business exist?
11. In what states and foreign countries does the business operate? Is it appropriately licensed and in good standing in each?
12. What percentage of the business may be owned by noncitizens of the home country?

163

General Questions to Answer Early:

1. What is the quality, competence, and depth of management?
2. Who are the *key* employees that must be retained?
3. What are the causes of any significant trends in revenues, profits, and ratios?
4. What have the cash flows been for the last five years?
5. Is there any portion of the current income stream that is likely to cease or be significantly reduced in the next five years?
6. Are there any revenue contracts? If so, when do they expire?
7. Are there any unusual or extraordinary expenses that are known or expected to occur in the next five years?
8. What were all capital expenditures during the last five years?
9. What is the current budget for capital expenditures?
10. Are there critical assets that must be replaced in the next five years?
11. Who controls the business? Who has voting power? Are there any coalitions of shareholders that must be approached?
12. What significant problems are known by current management?
13. Have attempts to sell the business been made before? If so, what are the details of each attempt?
14. Why is the business for sale?
15. Are there any subsidiaries being divested? If so, what are the details?
16. What employees are likely to leave if the sale is completed? Do any of these people have confidential information about such things as sales, customers, or projects that it is important to protect?
17. Is there any evidence of illegal activities, including, but not limited to, bribes, skimming, extortion, or embezzlement?
18. Is there any evidence of violations of law or regulations?
19. Has management "dressed up" the business by accelerating the recognition of revenues or decelerating the recognition of expenses?
20. What expenses may be eliminated if the business is purchased?

Capital Structure and Ownership:

1. What is the legal structure of the business?
2. How does this compare and contrast to U.S. legal structures?
3. How many shares are authorized and outstanding?
4. Is there more than one class of stock? If so, what are the details?
5. Has any of the stock traded during the business's existence?
6. Is the business in default on any loan or debt agreements?
7. Is any portion of the business's assets pledged as collateral for debt? If so, what are the details?

8. Are there any stock options, warrants, or pledges outstanding?
9. Have any employees been promised stock as a purchase, a bonus, in lieu of wages or salary, or as a bargain purchase, e.g., options or warrants?
10. What are the terms of the members of the board of directors?
11. In what way was each member elected to the board?
12. Are any willing to stay or any unwilling to resign if the business is purchased?

Management:

1. What is the total cost of the business's three top executives, including salary, bonus, expenses, options, severances, loans, and benefits?
2. To whom do employees look to make day-to-day decisions?
3. To whom do employees look to make major decisions?
4. Are there any currently unfilled executive positions?
5. What is the extent of nepotism in the business?
6. Who could severely damage the business if they left in hostile circumstances?
7. Are any executives or employees irreplaceable? Would their loss cause the failure of the business?
8. Are there any officers or salaried employees who work part-time, at home, or off business property?
9. Are there any officers, shareholders, directors, or employees who work for free or for very little pay? If so, what are the details?
10. Are any officers, consultants, or employees paid excessively for their duties and responsibilities? If so, what are the details?
11. Is there any evidence of conflict of interest on the part of any officers or key employees? If so, what are the details?
12. What benefits and perquisites do officers, directors, or consultants receive that are different from those provided for employees?
13. What is the reputation of management within the industry? Within the business by the employees?
14. Have any stockholders, officers, directors, or consultants been convicted of any crime, been involved in any scandals, or been part of any business that has failed?

Markets, Competition, and Customers:

1. What are the business's current markets?
2. Who are the business's customers? What are their ages, home places, businesses, gender, economic class, country of origin, and religion?
3. What is the business's share of each market served? What trends are there in market share?

4. Are there plans to enter new markets?

5. What competition exists for the products or services of the business?

6. Are any of the competitors expanding?

7. How does the business position its product or service—as a commodity, a luxury, or a value?

8. What is the business's unique competitive advantage over each competitor?

9. Is the business bound by any capacity or scheduling restrictions or regulations? Is the business bound by any noncompetition agreements?

10. What is the customers' opinion of the business?

Marketing:

1. What is the business's method of selling its product or service?

2. What percentage of the business's product or service is sold by agents?

3. What is the dollar volume of each product or service provided by the business?

4. Does the business have a formal, written marketing plan?

5. Have there been any major changes in marketing in the last two years?

6. What is the importance of the price of the product or service, its delivery terms, financing availability, and options?

7. What percentages of the product or service are paid for (a) by cash, check or money order, (b) by credit card, (c) on account, (d) in U.S. dollars, and (e) with other currencies?

8. Are any bribes paid to government or other officials at any level in the operations of the business?

9. How does demand respond to changes in product or service prices?

Scope of the Business:

1. What is the growth potential for the business?

2. What markets are underserved?

3. What new markets can be entered?

4. What is the revenue and cost of each market?

5. Are there any ongoing contracts with large customers?

6. What is the trend in (a) sales, (b) prices, (c) product costs, and (d) labor cost in each market served by the business?

7. Has the business ever had an accident or incident with injuries? If so, what were the circumstances?

8. Is the business's operating permit subject to renewal or expiration?

Long-Term Assets—Real Estate and Facilities:

1. What real estate and facilities does the business (a) own and (b) lease? What are the terms of the contracts?
2. Are any facilities for sale or lease? If so, why?
3. What is the efficiency of the business's use of the property? Is the facility operating at, over, or under capacity?
4. Are any negotiations underway to obtain any new or different facilities?
5. Are any facilities owned by shareholders, officers, directors, employees, or consultants? If so, are rents and contract provisions as favorable as if the facility was obtained from an outsider?
6. Does the business have clear title to owned properties?
7. Have any of the real estate or facilities been appraised for any reason?
8. Are current facilities adequate?
9. Are current facilities safe and secure from theft, vandalism, or terrorist attack?

Insurance and Liability Concerns:

1. What insurance(s) does the business carry? What are the cost and terms?
2. Is the business currently party to any lawsuits, judgments, garnishments, or financial claims?
3. What, if any, legal limits upon liability apply to the business?
4. Is the business subject to worker's compensation claims?

Short-Term Assets:

1. How much cash does the business have?
2. What is the value of accounts receivable?
3. What is the value of inventory?
4. What prepaid expenses does the business have?

Liabilities:

1. What are the nature and amounts of accounts payable?
2. Are accounts payable current? Are any currently being disputed?
3. Has the business ever been placed on a cash basis by any supplier because of nonpayment? Has the dispute been resolved?
4. What is the nature and amount of all taxes payable?
5. When must the outstanding taxes be paid?

6. Have any loans to the business been made by shareholders, officers, employees, consultants, or other insiders? If so, what are the details?

7. Does the business have a line of credit or other short-term borrowings?

8. Is the business subject to any judgment as a result of past litigation?

9. Does the business have any (a) outstanding bonds, (b) bank loans, or (c) long-term loans from any source? If so, what are the details?

10. What long-term leases does the business have?

11. Have any shareholders in the business made personal guarantees of any debt?

12. Is the business currently under investigation for any civil, criminal, or administrative issue?

References

Accounting Principles Board [APB]. *APB Opinion 29.* Stamford, CT: Financial Accounting Standards Board.

Accounting Research Bulletin [ARB]. *ARB No. 43.* Stamford, CT: Financial Accounting Standards Board.

Adams, J. S. (1963). Wage inequities, productivity and work quality. *Industrial Relations, 3.*

Alexander, G. J., Benson, P. G., & Gunderson, E. W. (1986). Asset redeployment: Trans World Corporation's spinoff of TWA. *Financial Management, 15*(2): 50-58.

Banks, H. (1994). Cleared for takeoff. *Forbes, 154*(6): 116-122.

Bennett, P. D. (Ed.). (1988). *Dictionary of marketing terms.* Chicago, IL: American Marketing Association.

Bradway, B. M., & Pritehard, R. E. (1980). *Developing the business plan for small business.* New York: Amacom.

Briers, M., Luckett, P., & Chow, C. (1997). Data fixation and the use of traditional versus activity-based costing systems. *Abacus, 33*(1): 49-68.

Castaneda, L. (1996, September 6). Packard Bell settles suit over used parts. *San Francisco Chronicle,* p. E1.

Coates, J. (1995, July 16). To the venerable typewriter, we say, ta-ta, tin keys. *Chicago Tribune,* Section 7, p. 5.

Collins, G. (1996, March 15). Heinz cutting 2,500 jobs in revamping. *New York Times,* pp. 21-22.

Cooked books fixed stew. (1993). *Retail World, 46*(17): 7.

Cooper, R. G. (1994a). Debunking the myths of new product development. *Research-Technology Management, 37*(4): 40-50.

Cooper, R. G. (1994b). New products: The factors that drive success. *International Marketing Review, 11*(1): 60-76.

Creese, R. (1993). Break-even analysis—the fixed quantity approach. *Transactions of the American Association of Cost Engineers,* pp. A.1.1-A.1.7.

Currid, C. (1995, August 21). The lesson of Smith Corona. *Informationweek, 21:* 88.

Dankner, H. (1981). *Employer accounting for pension costs and other post-retirement benefits.* New York: Financial Executives Research Foundation, Coopers & Lybrand.

Evans, J., & Berman, B. (1994). *Marketing* (6th ed.). Englewood Cliffs, NJ: Prentice Hall.

Fabrycky, W. J., Ghare, P. M., & Torgersen, P. E. (1984). *Applied operations research and management science.* Englewood Cliffs, NJ: Prentice Hall.

Felsenthal, E. (1997, May 13). High court backs workers on benefits. *Wall Street Journal,* p. A3.

Financial Accounting Standards Board [FASB]. (1996). Statements of concepts. *Original Pronouncements* (Vol. 2). Stamford, CT: Author.

Fleming, P. D. (1996). Insurance for business needs. *Journal of Accountancy, 181*(1): 61.

Francis, R. L., McGinnis, L. F., & White, J. A. (1992). *Facility layout and location: An analytical approach.* Englewood Cliffs, NJ: Prentice Hall.

Fry, F. L., & Stoner, C. L. (1985). Business plans: Two major types. *Journal of Small Business Management, 23*(1): 1-6.

Garrison, R. H. (1985). *Managerial accounting.* Plano, TX: Business Publications.

General aviation deliveries drop to record low in U.S. (1988). *Aviation Week & Space Technology, 128*(4): 137, 141.

Hawbaker, A. C., & Nixon, J. M. (1991). *Industry and company information: Illustrated search strategy and sources.* Ann Arbor, MI: Pierian Press.

Hefty, T. (1990). *Funding post-retirement health benefits: Who will pay?* Chicago, IL: Tort and Insurance Practice Section, American Bar Association.

Hesse, R., & Woolsey, G. (1980). *Applied management science: A quick and dirty approach.* Chicago, IL: Science Research Associates.

Hilton, R. W. (1994). *Managerial accounting* (2nd ed.). New York: McGraw-Hill.

Hirsch, M. L. (1993). Break-even analysis: Basic model, variants, extentions. *Accounting Review, 68*(1): 209-210.

Hoard, B. (1985). Ted Turner! *On Communications, 2*(1): 26-28.

Hoffer, W. (1987). Bloch that IRS return. *Nation's Business, 75*(3): 69-70.

Hooper, L., & Berton, L. (1991, March 29). IBM to record large charge for new rule. *Wall Street Journal,* p. A3.

Hudis, M., & Brower, A. (1993). Tie-ins. *Brandweek, 34*(22): 34.

Ingram, B. (1993). Stew, we hardly knew ye. *Supermarket Business, 48*(9): 167-168.

Insight Information. (1994). *Reducing post retirement benefit costs.* Toronto, Ontario: Insight Press.

Jarboe, G. R. (1996). *The marketing research project manual.* St. Paul, MN: West.

Kahrs, K., & Krek, K. (Eds.). (1998). *Business plans handbook: A compilation of actual business plans developed by small businesses throughout North America.* Detroit, MI: Gale Research.

Kaplan, R. S. (Ed.). (1990). *Measures for manufacturing excellence.* Boston: Harvard Business School Press.

Keys, P. (1991). *Operational research and systems: The systematic nature of operational research.* New York: Plenum.

Landry, S. P., Wood, L. M., & Lindquist, T. M. (1997). Can ABC bring mixed results? *Management Accounting, 78*(9): 28-33.

Levitt, T. (1986). *The marketing imagination.* New York: Free Press.

Magee, R. P. (1986). *Advanced managerial accounting.* New York: Harper & Row.

Mamis, R. A. (1989, March). Fatal attraction. *INC., 11*(3): 77-86.

McGarvey, J. (1996, September 26). Compaq pushes past Packard Bell [On-line]. *INTER@CTIVE WEEK.* World Wide Web: Ziff Davis Interactive, http://www.zdnet.com/intweek/daily.

McNair, C. J. (1993). *World-class accounting and finance.* Homewood, IL: Business One Irwin.

McShane, M. (1996). Insurance for small companies: A big problem. *Australian Accountant, 66*(10): 36-40.

Murdoch, J. (1998). Microsoft courts the little guy. *Visual Basic Programmer's Journal, 8*(8).

Niemann, H. F. C. (1990, February). Buying a business. *INC., 12*(2): 28-38.

Niemann, H. F. C. (1991, October). The rest of the story. *INC., 13*(10): 38-46.

Norkus, G., & Merberg, E. (1994). Food distribution in the 1990s. *Cornell Hotel & Restaurant Administration Quarterly, 35*(3): 50-63.

Posner, B. G., Brokaw, L., & Brown, P. B. (1990, July). Squeeze play: 40 ways to cut your losses. *INC., 12*(7): 68-75.

Pratt, S. P. (1989). *Valuing a business: The analysis and appraisal of closely held companies* (2nd ed.). Homewood, IL: Irwin Business One.

Ricchuite, D. N. (1995). *Auditing* (4th ed.). Cincinnati, OH: South-Western College.

Sandberg, J. (1997, September 4). H&R Block is close to sale of CompuServe stake. *Wall Street Journal*, p. A3.

Securities and Exchange Commission [SEC]. *Accounting series release 25*. Washington, DC: Author.

Securities and Exchange Commission [SEC]. (1978). *Accounting series release 253*. Washington, DC: Author.

Sellers, P. (1992, October). The dumbest marketing ploy. *Fortune, 126*(7): 88-94.

Shim, E., & Sudit, E. (1995). How manufacturers price products. *Management Accounting, 76*(8): 37-39.

Shocker, D., Stewart, W., and Zahorik, A. J. (1990). *Determining the competitive structure of product-markets: Practices, issues, and suggestions*. Cambridge, MA: Marketing Science Institute.

Stanford University. (1998). Midcom communications complaint [On-line]. *Securities class action clearinghouse*. World Wide Web: http://securities.stanford.edu/cv-96-614d.

Swartz, J. (1996, January 29). Apple's market share dwindles [On-line]. *MacWEEK News*. World Wide Web: Ziff Davis Interactive, http://macweek.zdnet.com/.

van der Laan, E., & Dekker, R. (1996). An (s, Q) inventory model with remanufacturing and disposal. *International Journal of Production Economics, 46-47*: 339-350.

Varadarajan, P. R. (1985). Joint sales promotion: An emerging marketing tool. *Business Horizons, 28*(5): 43-49.

Vijayan, J. (1995). Probe may beget reform. *Computerworld, 29*(30): 2.

Wing, M. J. (1997). *The Arthur Andersen guide to talking with your customers: What they will tell you about your business (when you ask the right questions)*. Chicago: Upstart.

Index

About the Authors

Richard P. Green II, Ph.D., CPA, operates a consulting business, established in 1982. Among his current clients is Land O' Lakes, for whom he does financial analyses of foreign dairy and food producers. He has owned several sign companies, including *Richard Green Sign Service,* which, at age 18, he started in Springfield, Missouri. He has been a pilot for Trans World Airlines and held a position with the Air Line Pilots' Association; has owned controlling interest in Western Steel, Inc., and minority interests in two Missouri banks; and has operated a land development and house building company. For his consulting business, he wrote a program for the MAI Basic 4 computer to calculate federal, Missouri, and Kansas income taxes, which he used in the conduct of a tax preparation business. In the fall of 1990, he resigned his position with the Air Line Pilots' Association and sold his various business interests. Since then he has completed a master's degree in accounting at the University of Missouri—St. Louis, and a Ph.D. in business administration at St. Louis University.

James J. Carroll, Ph.D., is Professor of Business Administration at Georgian Court College, Lakewood, New Jersey. He also holds professional designations as a CMA, CPA, and CFE. He has degrees from New Jersey Institute of Technology (BSIE), Rutgers University (MBA-Finance), and Nova Southeastern University (DBA-Management). He is currently on the editorial board of the *Journal of Small Business Management* and the *Case Research Journal,* and has served on the boards for the *Journal of Managerial Issues* and the *Journal of Small Business Strategy.*

He has received the Leavey Award (1987) and the Freedoms Foundation of Valley Forge Award (1986) for Excellence in Education, and the first Best Reviewer award ever issued from the *Journal of Small Business Management* (1996). His publications include articles in *The Academy of Management Executive*, textbooks on entrepreneurship and accounting, and examinations for U.S. accounting certification. He has served as Chief Financial Officer for divisions of *Fortune* 500 companies, leveraged-buyout companies, and not-for-profit organizations. He is an active forensic consultant, having provided more than 125 written opinions and testified in more than 25 legal matters.

Investigating Entrepreneurial Opportunities is a practical, comprehensive guide to the critical due diligence process of determining whether or not to acquire a business. Entrepreneurs and students of entrepreneurship alike will find its step-by-step instructions not only thorough but also easy to follow. The authors plumb their own real-world experience to cover in depth all the investigative basics, including markets, products, insurance, facilities, assets, short- and long-term liabilities, and much more. They reveal creative, low-cost ways to conduct your own due diligence process and offer insider tips such as how to uncover hidden assets and unrecorded liabilities. The book provides handy checklists of "tasks to be completed" and "questions to be answered" during the exercise of due diligence.

Drs. Green and Carroll are both not only educators but also experienced businessmen. Both are CPAs who have themselves conducted hundreds of due diligence assignments. Their collaborative effort offers the reader a street-smart view of business start-ups and acquisitions that is grounded in general theory and transferable to all types of entrepreneurial endeavors. Anyone who is considering acquiring or starting a business of any kind in the near or distant future can benefit from owning this book.

Entrepreneurship and the Management of Growing Enterprises
ISBN: 0-8039-5941-9 hardcover
ISBN: 0-8039-5942-7 paperback

Visit our website at www.sagepub.com

ISBN 0-8039-5942-7

780803   959422

90000>

SAGE Publications
International Educational and Professional Publisher
Thousand Oaks   London   New Delhi

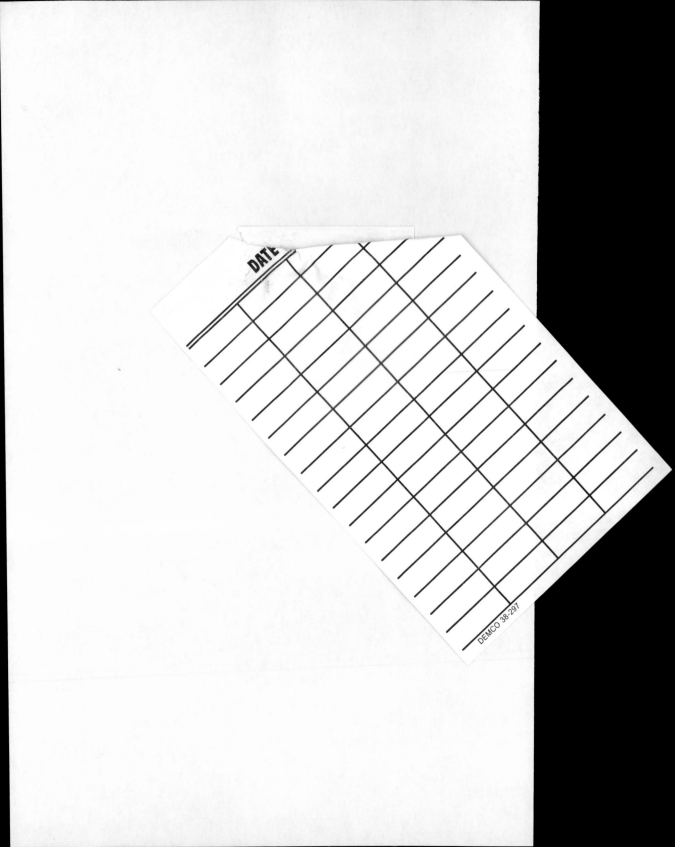

DATE

DEMCO 38-297